the Joy of Walking

More Than Just Exercise

Stephen Christopher Joyner

920414

BETTERWAY PUBLICATIONS, INC.

WHITE HALL, VIRGINIA

206 South Market
Marion, Illinois 62959

Published by Betterway Publications, Inc.
P.O. Box 219
Crozet, VA 22932
(804) 823-5661

Cover design and photograph by Susan Riley
Photographs by Paul McCallum
Typography by East Coast Typography, Inc.

Library of Congress Cataloging-in-Publication Data

Joyner, Stephen Christopher
    The joy of walking : more than just exercise / Stephen Christopher Joyner.
        p.   cm.
        Includes bibliographical references (p.) and index.
        ISBN 1-55870-232-6 : $9.95
    1. Walking.   I. Title.
GV502.J69   1992
613.7'176–dc20

91-43800
CIP

Printed in the United States of America
0 9 8 7 6 5 4 3 2 1

This book is gratefully dedicated to
The Members of the First and Second Triad.

Pullen Warwick Portney

●

Converse Converse Converse

Your efforts have saved a precious life.
I am forever in your debt.

Contents

In the middle of the journey of our life
I found myself in a dark wood,
For I had lost the right path . . .

Dante

There was a child went forth every day,
And the first object he look'd upon, that
Object he became . . .

Walt Whitman

CHAPTER 1

Why Walk?

'Tis the best of humanity that comes out to walk.
Ralph Waldo Emerson

And what a wide, wonderful world it is for walking, with few boundaries because little terrain is off-limits. You can walk through the world as though it were your own village.

In the walker's world there is no tyranny of the calendar, no one season for walking. It is a year-round pleasure, with each season offering its own special gifts. In winter, when the whole earth is in repose and the air nips at the skin, a walk is just as enjoyable as it is on a summer night, with its aura of intrigue and mystery, or on a spring day, when the earth is vibrant in its wakening freshness.

To this, add one more compelling fact: every city in America still leads out into wide open spaces. The variety of experiences open to the walker is limitless!

Indeed, America is a walker's paradise full of mystery, joy, and wonderment. My walks have always been a very special pleasure. Like so many of us, I, too, am often preoccupied with my job and daily responsibilities. Yet, I rarely cheat myself and forgo an energizing walk. To do so would be to jeopardize my daily peace and productivity.

Each morning I awake a couple hours before my day has to begin, put on my walking shoes, and head for the hills of San Francisco. My brisk walks up Lombard Street are exhausting indeed, but I so savor the euphoric high that envelops me after I've showered and dressed for the day that I don't mind the extra sweat, effort, and concentration. Having reached the plateau, I am rewarded when catalyzing enzymes invigorate my body.

FOOTSTEPS

- In about 20% of the population, the second toe is the longest.
- Each pair of feet is composed of 52 bones. That is one-fourth of all those in the body.
- An average person takes 6,000 to 8,000 steps each day.
- The largest men's shoes ever sold were worn by Harley Davidson. His size — 42.

Let's face it, our feet were made for walking. Thomas Jefferson wrote, "Walking is the best exercise of all." Almost 200 years have passed since he uttered those words, and modern physiologists are, once again, prescribing this most basic exercise.

But why now? Well, for one thing, it is one of the best forms of exercise, and with the increasing emphasis on fitness and health pervading nearly every facet of our lives, it is understandable that more and more Americans are taking to their feet to experience the easy, inexpensive, low-impact exercise that keeps their bodies toned and minds sharp.

But walking is so much more. Come with me. Let's take a walk . . .

❢ WALKING IS EASY

When I suggest to people that they walk as a form of exercise, they usually look at me in disbelief, with a half-cracked smile, or at least with the implication that walking is just, well, walking!

The fact that walking is easy does not make it an illegitimate exercise. Actually, mile for mile you burn as many calories walking (about 100 calories per mile) as you do jogging, without the contorted face muscles, the pounding of the bones and joints, and the pain of runner's fatigue. Al-

1. *Just about anyone can walk.*

though the simple pleasure of walking has been overshadowed by glamorous and expensive sports such as tennis, skiing, and scuba diving, its rewards — and they are many — can be equal to those of many other forms of exercise.

It requires no more than a pair of shoes (preferably walking shoes), some comfortable clothes, and a little common sense. Walking is more than a sport, more than an exercise. It is a way of life for men and women of all ages. We were born to walk. Walking is both our achievement and our heritage. And it is easy!

❗ *WALKING REDUCES HEART DISEASE*

"The mechanization of America, . . . [most notably] the invention of the elevator, the motor car, and the television, has reduced the majority of our population to a sedentary lifestyle," said Dr. Albert A. Kattus in 1974, when he was chairman of the Exercise Committee of the American Heart Association. Today's lifestyle has a great deal to do with the development of arteriosclerosis, the clogging of the arteries of the heart, brain, and kidneys. Arteriosclerosis kills and cripples more people than all other diseases combined. What an irony of our age that this scourge of the human race is self-inflicted!

Indeed, it is — but we can do something to change it. Walking benefits the heart by making it work harder and, ultimately, more efficiently. With a continuous walking regimen (or any other sustained aerobic exercise), the heart can pump more blood with less effort. With more time to rest between beats, you can exercise for longer periods of time without getting tired and respond to physical and emotional crises without exerting your heart, pulsing your veins with blood, and raising your blood pressure.

❗ *WALKING TAKES THE WEIGHT OFF*

Weight loss is easy to understand. The food you eat is potential energy, and your body has two options — to burn up this energy or to store it as fat. Inactivity is generally considered to be the most important factor in explaining the preponderance of overweight people in our society. Fat adults and children are less physically active than people of normal body weight. There are so many things we have no control over in our lives, but being slim or fat is not one of them. You decide.

To slim down and stay that way, you don't have to go on absurd milk shake diet plans or fast for weeks at a time. Instead, consider that walking is the most sensible way to lose weight and keep it off.

Controlling your weight will not only maintain your health and a youthful countenance, but it also goes a long way toward keeping you alive. Research studies show a close relationship between weight and longevity.

❗ *WALKING SLOWS DOWN THE AGING PROCESS*

Does walking actually increase your life span? Well, maybe. But many doctors do believe that a daily walk can help you remain in a youthful condition.

Doubtless, your body will become brittle and sluggish if you don't use it. The result will be slow circulation; thin, porous bones; and weakened muscles. Walking is an easy way to fight the aging process. Exercised bones don't demineralize and are far less likely to break. Every muscle in your body is exercised when you walk. Walking nurtures, refreshes, and rebuilds the body despite its programmed deterioration. You can defer the inevitable, and stay young and healthy, by walking regularly.

❢ WALKING REHABILITATES

Walking helps speed recovery from many types of injuries, especially those in the upper body. Typically, walking is not recommended for lower body injuries, and, in any event, your doctor's endorsement is strongly advised. For some time, recovering heart attack patients were advised to avoid exercise. Today, however, walking is an important part of all cardiac rehab programs. Typically, patients rehabilitating from heart surgery, and those in the later stages of rehabilitation from hip and leg operations, are advised to walk indoors. Since extreme temperatures can exert the recovery patient, many malls across the country sponsor pre-opening/post-closing walking programs where the temperature is controlled.

❢ WALKING IMPROVES MENTAL HEALTH

Tension, anxiety, stress, depression. Each of us encounters emotional stressors in our life from time to time. This causes a tremendous energy drain and may ultimately lead to high blood pressure. Mental illness also contributes to obesity, ulcers, colitis, muscular twitches, heart disease, cancer, emotional disorders, depression, and various compulsions. A vigorous walk, however, increases your "oxygen transport capacity" — the amount of oxygen that each heartbeat delivers to the rest of the body. Mental alertness and mood improve when larger amounts of pure oxygen are delivered to the brain cells.

Indeed, walkers are usually more stable emotionally than non-walkers. I just find it extremely difficult to walk rapidly and brood at the same time. If you make it a point to walk every day, your morale and productivity will improve.

I remember reading an old comedy routine about a doctor who steps on his patient's foot to make the patient forget about his headache. I believe there is something of that in the relationship between walking and mental well-being. Walkers are forced to notice new and significant sensations that distract them from their worldly worries. Intense concentration demands that you escape for a period of time. And walking is a form of escape, which is precisely why, when we feel a crisis bearing down on us, we often get to our feet and pace the room. We can and must escape if we are to remain sane and clear-minded.

STRESS RELIEF

Your ability to manage stress affects your mental and physical health. Too much stress can lead to high blood pressure, heart disease, depression, schizophrenia, indigestion, increased cholesterol, stilted concentration, low back pain, headaches, cancer, and a lower resistance to pain. Too little stress is also harmful. It may contribute to boredom, loneliness, depression, and possibly suicide.

We adapt best to stress in the middle of the extremes. Positive stress enhances our ability to perform by helping us to overcome laziness and motivating us to be productive and excel. As with many things in life, moderation is best. Ideally, one's level of stress should be somewhere between having too much to do and being completely bored.

A healthy strategy for dealing with too much stress is regular exercise. Walking helps release muscular tension by alternating and rhythmically contracting your muscles. Like all sustained aerobic exercises, walking leaves a lingering sensation of calm and vitality.

Sustained aerobic walking simulates a mini-vacation and gives you a respite from the pressures of the day. Walking provides a time to be by yourself or with others, depending on what best suits you. Regular walkers report that their fitness walk helps them cope with relationships, expectations of others, and financial difficulties.

Walking remains the safest, most effortless way to rid yourself of anger and anxiety that I know of. Any aerobic exercise is superior to the stop-and-go sports of basketball or tennis (and far superior to a bruising physical contact sport), yet I find that no sport reduces stress-related tension as effectively and safely as walking does.

IMPROVES SELF-ESTEEM

As emotional beings, we all have a need for strong self-esteem. This includes a feeling of personal worth, success, achievement, internal love, and a fulfilling occupation in life. Although sometimes left adrift in the haze of youth, we can and must take pride in feeling healthy and looking good in years to come.

A regular walking routine builds self-esteem. There is a scientifically proven correlation between physical fitness and emotional well-being. Sticking with a regular fitness plan develops self-discipline, which engenders feelings of accomplishment and self-worth. Each time you get up early, stretch, and go on a walk, you achieve a personal victory over laziness and low self-respect. Moreover, the positive physical development that results from your walking program contributes to increased self-confidence. Indeed, looking good is feeling good.

Above all, believe in yourself and your abilities. Get out and walk each day. Let everything in your life grow and expand from the inherent simplicity of walking. Combined with proper nutrition and adequate rest, your modest, daily journey into the world will help you accomplish your goals in life.

IMPROVES CREATIVE ABILITIES

Good mental health allows you to become a better problem-solver. Like most aerobic exercises, walking stimulates an increase in the oxygen supply to the brain. Consequently, this improves our cognitive abilities, memory retention, concentration, and clarity of thought.

To further your benefit, try varying your walking routes. Some walkers, myself included, theorize that you can train yourself to think more creatively. By viewing the external world with forward motion and the resulting increase in enzyme production, you may begin to interpret things as you never have. Look around with an increased interest in the sights and sounds that stimulate pleasurable emotional and mental reactions — the sounds of park sprinklers, shoreline breakers, or resonating city streets. These mental exercises, coupled with the enhanced energy from walking, help you overcome your problems and conceive of solutions that the resting body has no access to.

WALK TO WORK

May is National Physical Fitness and Sports Month. In 1992, the third National Employee Health and Fitness Day will be held to encourage companies to promote exercise at and commuting to the workplace.

For an information pack, company activity directors may contact the National Association of Governors' Council on Fitness and Sports, Pan American Plaza, 201 South Capital Avenue, Suite 440, Indianapolis, IN 46225 (317) 237-5630.

INCREASES YOUR SENSE OF WELL-BEING

A regular walking program increases the brain's supply of endorphins, which function as the body's natural opiates. They work to lower the body's sensation of pain and provide an overall sense of well-being. Studies indicate that regular exercise increases the flow of these endorphins to the brain and keeps them there longer. The moderate amount of endorphins released during fitness walking produces feelings of energy, strength, hope, and inner peace.

For a period of two years, I struggled through a difficult depression. A typical symptom of depression is to "hibernate" — to withdraw completely from society and friends. There were days, however, when the black cloud lurking overhead would move just enough to allow me to escape my apartment/cell and breathe the fresh air of San Francisco. Having conquered the illness, I am particularly empathetic to despondent people in and about my life, and I am always amazed how often depressed people walk without having been told to. I think the body is driven to it. If you let it, your body will dictate what is best for you and what is not. I believe that for reactive depressions there is no exercise better than walking.

❗ *WALKING ENDS BOREDOM*

Boredom is a feeling of fundamental indifference to life. Lack of change, of excitement, and of responsibilities may contribute to stress and depression. Unfulfilling work, sometimes coupled with an unfulfilling or a dead-end relationship, undermines your feeling of control and ability to change your life. Allowed to persist, boredom may be the initial symptom of a full-scale depression.

As suggested throughout *The Joy of Walking,* a walk yields new vistas and perspectives to your life. When I feel hopelessly adrift and bored with my life, it's difficult to get out of bed in the morning. During these periods, nothing feels good. In my torpid indifference, I view my home as a cell block. It becomes a perennial reminder that time — moving at a glacial pace — is being served. It adds to a feeling of life escaping me, or vice versa. However, with all my strength, somehow I remind myself that there is an effective elixir, and I force myself out into the world. Almost without fail, my mood improves.

On my feet and moving against the current of the breeze, my mind is stimulated to think about improving my life. When I walk, I find it quite difficult to be depressed. Next time you are struck by a spell of boredom or indifference, try taking a walk!

❗ *WALKING STIMULATES YOUR MIND*

"Methinks that the moment my legs begin to move, my thoughts begin to flow." Enveloped in the serenity of Walden Pond, Henry David Thoreau capsulizes the therapeutic benefit of walking.

Your body thrives on the movement of blood and oxygen. Through aerobic exercise you increase the enzyme production and blood flow to your central nervous system and brain. As your brain receives more enzymes, your creative and problem-solving capacities increase, and the mind becomes alive and free from unproductive worry and torpor, which is doubtless compounded by sitting around or watching anesthetizing, prime-time pseudodrama. (I don't care for television.)

❗ *YOU SEE DIFFERENTLY WHEN YOU WALK*

In the October 1978 edition of *National Geographic,* Carolyn Patterson said of walking: "My extraordinary new awareness of the land and the animals, [was] opened by the pace of walking. I feel that I am literally seeing everything for the first time." Walking in rhythmic motion, with the arms and legs swinging in concert, frees the mind and stimulates an acute sense of sight and sound, which gives the walker access to a different world.

In our daily lives we tend to drive through our environment at great speeds. Eyes looking far and forward, cocooned in cars with stereo and climate control, we know not what passes our shoulders. To really come to know your neighborhood, your city, or your vacation spot, you must put the vehicle in park, put your feet on solid ground, and rev up your senses to see and to feel those sights and sounds that typically pass you by.

The only true Americans, the American Indians, held that man is not outside of nature, but actually of it. In other words, nature is a phenomenon of which we are a part. Experience it. Feel it. Touch the ground, the trees. Feel the wind and the cold and the rain. As your senses awaken, a feeling of well-being will emerge. Walk erect, breathe deeply, really look around and within yourself. Feel the world around you, and you will see everything about you as though it were for the first time.

❢ WALKING IS FUN WITH OTHERS

> *Don't walk in front of me, I might not follow.*
> *Don't walk behind me, I might not lead.*
> *Walk beside me, And be my friend.*
>
> Allison Atlas
> December 1986

Walking with another human being is wonderful. A walk after dinner is especially gratifying, analagous to a pedestrian form of an after-dinner brandy. Indeed, I can think of no other exercise during which you can have a sustained and engaging conversation.

Some of the best discussions I have had with friends and lovers have been while walking. You can walk and talk or walk together in happy silence, letting your closeness and the perfect rhythm of the walk you are sharing speak for the two

2. *Walking with someone is perhaps the finest aspect of walking.*

3. *A walk with Kiwi on a Sunday afternoon.*

of you. You may hold hands or link arms; lead, follow, or walk as one.

I believe that walking with someone you like or want to get to know on any level is the surest way to get to know that person better. Sharing a walk is much like sharing food. It is so simple, basic, and pure.

A WALK WITH YOUR DOG

I've never cared much for the expression "walking the dog." You don't walk a dog any more than you walk a child. You walk *with* a dog like the loyal friend he is.

Just thinking of the euphemisms used for dogs sounds a chord: "man's best friend," "my forever friend," "that smart dog of mine," "my pal." Again and again man feels enormous affection for and closeness to his dog.

Dogs, like small children, seem to know when a walk is an act of love and not an act of obligation. And if the walk is in open spaces and your dog can be free of the leash, notice that he assumes the role not only of companion but also of protector. Walking in the hills of San Francisco with my collie, Pushkin, I see a change in his attitude. It is as though our roles reverse now that we are out of domestic confines and walking through an open, unfamiliar territory. In such an environment, I become the particular concern of Pushkin, who runs ahead, turns around, and checks on my progress; then, convinced all is safe, he leads me onward just as any trusted guide might. I enjoy my walks with Pushkin no less than I do those I take with my two-legged friends.

A CHILD AND HIS DOG

I wish every child could know the delight of walking with a dog. A good dog has a kind of natural dignity that is never so evident as it is when he is walking in free, open spaces. We adults see this, but small children sense it and respond in the same way they do to the great majesty of a giant Sequoia or a towering waterfall. The child and the animal are both innocent, unspoiled spirits, and they respond to each other in a way that our jaded, evolved adulthood makes quite impossible. Adults should envy this unique kinship and work at every opportunity to encourage its growth.

❕ WALKING IS INEXPENSIVE

What could be less expensive than walking? Put on a pair of walking shoes, and you're off! Indeed, there are few forms of exercise that are as simple and inexpensive as walking. After all, we walk wherever we are. Walking is more than an exercise; it is a way of life.

And if walking becomes a daily ritual for you, then some inexpensive accessories will enhance your walk further. You might consider one or more of the following: a ball to bounce as you walk through dull terrain; a pedometer to keep track of your progress; a Walkman™ to play your favorite music; a walking stick to aid your rhythm, stability, and protection; a water bottle so you can remain hydrated; a small backpack to tote some high-energy food; and some extra clothing. Walking is one of the least expensive forms of exercise, even when you are fully outfitted.

❗ *EVERYONE CAN WALK*

In the past, people who had had heart attacks, suffered from emphysema or arthritis, or were extraordinarily overweight were prescribed medicine and rest. Now, doctors are now telling their patients "to get some exercise" — and with greater frequency, to get out and walk.

It makes sense! What other activity is so well suited to those with medical problems? Jogging? Too stressful on the ailing organs. Golf? No significant cardiovascular benefit. Cycling? Hardened bones cannot endure the wide pedal revolutions.

But walking! Now here's an exercise, a social activity, and a real joy of a sport that practically anyone can do. Young or old, heavyset or lean, strong or weak, man or woman, boy or girl — walking is here for everyone, at any time.

❗ *ARE YOU READY?*

Then let's get on with our journey through *The Joy of Walking* and become a free member of The New Walking Awareness.

4. A walk in the park on a Sunday. Walking is proven to improve your mood.

Get out on the road! Keep your legs, arms, and lungs healthy and limber. Pump up your flattened chests with God's free air. Warm your blood. Start it coursing through your brain. Purify your weathered skin with honest sweat. Throw away your cigarettes and smash your cocktail glasses. Leave the subways and the buses, the trolley cars and the autos to couch potatoes and other torpid souls. Don't be afraid of the rain and the wind. They have their parts to play in nature, just as the sunshine has. Walking has no seasons — no occasion to duck into anonymity. And now, neither do you!

CHAPTER 2

Getting Started

Walking is man's best medicine.
Hippocrates

❢ *WHAT IS WALKING?*

Walking is nothing more than a series of controlled, forward falls; a dance of the feet — just one foot in front of the other.

How could something so inherently simplistic command such a following, presently estimated at seventy-five million people? Indeed, walking ranks number one among forty sports and fitness activities. Nearly a quarter of the nation strides to the wonderful benefits of walking.

So take to your feet. It sounds simple enough. Just lace on some shoes and walk. But wait a minute. Before jumping to your feet, some prudent planning will maximize your safety and ultimate joy of walking.

❢ *BASICS TO REMEMBER*

Before you begin walking, consider your overall health and develop a walking program. Don't skip any steps in your hurry to take the first step! Many of these tips will be covered in detail in later chapters, but here is a summary of the main points.

CONSULT WITH YOUR PHYSICIAN

This is primarily for those over thirty. Beginning at age twenty-five, the body turns off the trail of growth and begins to amble down the road of deterioration. Slam on the brakes! You need to begin exercising with greater awareness than ever to slow the aging process.

STRETCHING

Stretching is an essential component of any exercise, and walking is no exception. A stretching routine helps your body develop and maintain flexibility.

Because stretching is most effective when the body is warm, walk easily for about ten minutes before you begin. You can also take a hot shower if this is more convenient. (See Chapter 3 for more details on stretching.)

SAFETY

Walking with a friend is always a good idea. Also, always carry identification, a house key, some cash or a credit card, and medication, if there is any you may require. If you do not have any pockets, wear a fanny pack or obtain a plastic ID pouch and loop the contents around your neck with a shoelace.

WALK IN WALKING SHOES

Would you wear golf shoes to bowl? How about a pair of ice skates for racketball? Of course not! Then why on earth walk in running shoes?

Depending on the speed and stride, a runner may run with a heel-toe motion, flatfooted, or on the ball of the foot. However, a walker always lands on the heel and slowly rolls the weight forward to the ball of the foot. Basically, the mechanics of running are completely different from those of walking.

A true walking shoe must be built with leather and other long-lasting materials to provide support in addition to durability.

5. *A good pair of walking shoes will take you a long way in good comfort.*

Running shoes are designed to absorb greater shock than are walking shoes, and they have less room for the toes to move and breathe. In addition, the soles have a smaller footprint and are less stable than those of walking shoes.

‼ DEVELOP A WALKING SCHEDULE

A walking schedule will aid you as you make your first venture into fitness walking. You will want to keep a record of your progress — both cardiovascular and weight loss, if that is your primary interest. On the road to greater fitness, however, I am confident that you will discover the many other benefits walking has to offer. Some, I confess, are less tangible than others; but they will augment your greater wellness just the same.

As you launch your walking program, concentrate more on the time walked and not so much on the distance covered. Initially, achieving aerobic physical health requires at least twenty minutes of sustained walking. Also, twenty minutes of walking will give you time to reflect on whatever is preoccupying you at the moment — your schedule, an argument with a friend, a deadline at work — as well as wake you up.

Morning walks are best since there are just too many things vying for your time later in the day. Walking (or any other health program) must become your number one priority, so it should have the top spot on your daily agenda. Think of it as your morning "triple-cappuccino-something" that will give you all the zest, verve, and adrenalin you need for the day.

Later, when you feel comfortable (breathing is easier, you are more limber, and you do not experience ongoing foot fatigue), increase your time walking by half-hour increments. If you experience any discomfort, continue with just twenty minutes. If foot pain persists, begin regular home foot treatment or seek a referral for a reputable podiatrist in your area. (See Chapter 9.)

Ultimately, your goal should be to walk your determined mileage four days a week. As you become more fit, you will have to increase your pace to reach your target heart rate. Build your pace gradually. As your speed increases and your stride follows, your distance will increase, your breathing rate will slow, and your body will assume full control of the walking, thus freeing your mind to take a "walk" all on its own.

I find that I go on "cruise control" and become unaware of the physical walking itself. This, I believe, is another of walking's greatest joys. When we can explore the world around or within ourselves without distractions, walking serves as a conduit to our greatest creative and problem-solving capacities.

❢ KEEP TRACK OF YOUR PROGRESS

To measure your mileage, select a landmark and regularly compare your time at that location (a tree, a building, or something more interesting). Or you can simplify this process and purchase a pedometer, a sophisticated device that accounts for your time, mileage, and caloric expenditure. Strap the pedometer around your waist prior to your walk and be off on your way. A pedometer's greatest attribute is that it allows you the freedom to choose your route impulsively as you go, while recording each step you take.

For best results, use the *Recipe of Four:* walk four times a week, for one hour, at four miles per hour. As you accomplish your established goals, unleash yourself and walk wherever, whenever, and for as long as you like.

❢ DEVELOP A WALKING ATTITUDE

Your walking success hinges on your personality, discipline, and attitude. Think back a moment to the last time you embarked on a fitness program. How long did it last? Alas, the

6. *The Trainer 350 pedometer records distance, counts calories, tracks walking time and miles walked, and has a scorekeeping function. About $40 by Sportline. (Photo by Steve Joyner.)*

statistics are against you sticking with anything that is good for your health. Chronic Fitness Dropout, as we will call it, is attributed to people with good intentions, who are tired of looking at the flab, but who cannot seem to stick with an exercise program. These are the people who join the fitness centers, purchase the "VIP Plan" for a small fortune, drop out after the first month, but appease their guilt by saying, "I'm a member of The Club." A typical response is, "Oh yes, I am too. Why don't I ever see you there?"

Indeed, nearly 50% of people who start a fitness program drop out within six months. Only a scant 20% of the U.S. population exercises regularly enough to stay fit. It takes more than good intentions or New Year's resolutions to stay fit.

Part of the problem is buried in the myth that many impatient people buy into — The Quick Fix Fitness Program. The Madison Avenue advertising artist knows you well and knows that you will buy into the "Sixty-Day Program." This is a short-term gimmick. Do not buy into it. Fitness is a lifelong proposition. It requires a program that you can stick with for the rest of your life, that you can do anywhere, at any time.

❗ EXCUSES, EXCUSES . . . I'VE HEARD THEM ALL!

Lest you have forgotten, great things do not happen overnight. You will come across obstacles. Here are some suggestions to conquer them.

ALERT: DON'T BE RASH THIS SUMMER

Both poison ivy, found in all states except California and Nevada, and poison oak, native to Washington, Oregon, and California, can grow as a conventional shrub or as an ornamental vine.

To avoid these scoundrel plants, look for shiny leaves in groups of three. Wear long clothing, leave the dog at home, wash hands frequently, and wash all clothing as soon as possible, including sneakers and hat. Clean hiking boots with rubbing alcohol.

If you are infected, prescribed hydrocortisone is most effective if applied immediately after infection is noticed. Until you can get some prescription-strength medicine, try using cold oatmeal or calamine lotion to prevent itching.

Be courteous and don't shake anyone's hands until you are cured.

No time. You already have a life. If walking interferes with family or work, map out a plan together. Your health and well-being must come before anything else. Think about that for a moment. Then decide if you agree with me.

It's boring. Alternate your routes. Vary your routine. Carry a Walkman™ and listen to your favorite tape or the news. Bounce a tennis ball. (Seriously!) It not only helps you with your rhythm, but will free your mind to concentrate and allow you to reach new levels of cognizance.

Think about something. Before you realize it, you will have covered a great deal of ground. Set out with a problem that needs solving. Walking, by stimulating norepinephrine and other enzymes in the brain, stimulates the mind and increases your ability to solve problems better than simply sitting behind a desk and pondering them.

I'm too tired after work. Walk in the morning. Ideally, your day should begin with exercise. You will find that you no longer need caffeine when you produce your body's own natural stimulants with exercise. If you are not able to walk in the morning, then walk at the end of your day, but don't relax and have a cocktail until after you have walked. Without discipline, you will not get off on the right foot.

It hurts. Pain means you are exercising too hard or not stretching adequately. Slow down and build gradually. If you are suddenly demanding that your body do something you have not allowed it to do in years, you are going to be sore after initial walks. But stay with it.

If pain persists, consult your physician or podiatrist. But beware of information you read or walking antagonists who tell you walking is bad for the feet. Most of us put socks on our feet in the morning and forget them. They carry our bodies around for a lifetime and most people rarely even give them powder or lotion. If your feet do hurt, good! It is about time you realized that more severe pain and injury lurk ahead if you don't begin giving your feet attention.

I am a younger walker, and my podiatrist determined that I have arthritis in my toes and arches — symptoms of a sixty year old! Why? I never bothered to get my feet examined when they gave me some mild pain over ten years ago. Please, do not assume that when your feet hurt on a regular basis, it is due to walking or being on them too much. See a podiatrist fast!

It's inconvenient. Nonsense! Going to the gym is inconvenient; you have to worry about driving, coping with traffic, parking! Put your walking shoes on and step out the front door.

I don't lose weight. Remember, there is more to walking than losing weight. But don't be surprised if you initially *gain* weight. As you burn fat, your body is replacing it with muscle, which weighs more.

You may also be fooling yourself if you believe you can eat more junk food or snacks as a reward for a hard workout. Have a banana or some other fresh fruit if you crave a sweet reward, but don't be counter-productive to your exercising with your diet — diet and exercise work together as one.

I get discouraged. Walk with someone. Walk with the dog. Join a walking club. Better yet, start one. Knowing other people are expecting you to walk with them is a great motivator.

❗ *OVERCOMING SETBACKS AND PROBLEMS WITH WALKING*

"Above all, do not lose your desire to walk every day. I walk myself into a state of well-being and walk away from every illness. I have walked myself into my best thoughts and I know of no thought so burdensome that I cannot walk away from it." As he wrote here, the Danish philosopher Kierkegaard believed strongly in the benefits of walking. But not every day you start to walk will you feel motivated and good about yourself. Don't let that stop you, though. Following are some obstacles you may run into, and some possible solutions to help you overcome those obstacles.

You just can't get going. Your legs feel like lead. Your arms don't swing well. You feel horrible. You thought exercise was supposed to invigorate you. What is happening? It is called *oxygen debt*. As you set out and your pace picks up, your muscles demand more blood and oxygen than your body can quickly supply. The result is that you feel sluggish. It may seem to last forever, but it will usually pass within five minutes or so. Just stick with it. Most of us have more patience with old, temperamental cars than we do with our own bodies.

You expect too much too soon. This is a common occurrence in all sports, and walking is no exception. I always had this problem with baseball until I dedicated myself to improving. It took time.

After about three weeks you should notice an improvement in your aerobic fitness. A mean way to test your progress is to ask a friend, one who does not exercise regularly, to go on a walk with you. Start talking and go up a hill or two; as your friend gasps, you won't feel so negative about your own improvement!

You stride longer to increase your speed. This is a walking myth. It is also a way to throw your back out or ruin your posture over time. Remember, your body was made to walk. Trust it to do so on its own terms.

Your body has a way of selecting what the appropriate stride is for any given walking speed. If your stride seems short, your higher rate of footfall will compensate. If you go against your body, if you decide how long to stride, you will be fighting gravity. Relax and let your legs do the walking.

You try to lose weight from a specific area of your body. Another exercise myth is spot reduction. When you walk, your body burns calories and fat proportionate to your *entire* body. The first step in shaping specific areas is to lose the weight. After that you can tone these areas through resistance training.

Done with devotion and love, your walks will move you into a greater joy and further away from a day when you can walk no more.

CHAPTER 3

Stretching

*I wish I could impress upon everybody that there
is no exercise more dignified or less expensive
or more conducive to health than walking.*
Edward Payson Weston

❗ WHY STRETCH?

There are many reasons to stretch. Following are some of the most important. Stretching:

- Prevents injuries such as muscle strains. (A strong, stretched muscle is resilient and less likely to tear.)

- Reduces muscle tension and makes the body feel more relaxed.

- Prepares you for strenuous activity. It's a way of signaling the muscles that they are about to be used.

- Helps coordination by allowing for freer and easier movement.

- Increases your range of motion.

- Promotes circulation of blood and oxygen.

- Helps to relax the mind's control over the body.

- Develops body awareness. As you stretch parts of the body, you focus on them and begin to "know" them and their limitations.

- Feels good!

Think of your body as a car that has been sitting in the garage overnight. When you start your car in the morning (especially if it is an older car) you need to give it time to warm up.

Your body is no different. Warm-up exercises and stretches should be performed slowly and steadily. By stretching, you awaken the muscles and warm them up, thus making them more resistent to unintentional twists or falls you may encounter on your walk.

Warm-ups and cool-downs also provide psychological benefits for walkers. You can use the warm-up time to prepare mentally for the walk you are about to take or to grade your performance on the one you have just completed. Focus on your form, time, and stamina. Or focus on nothing at all and put on some music. Some of the stretches can be done while watching television, talking on the phone, or lying in bed.

Ideally, everyone who takes a walk, whether it be a leisurely stroll or an all-out sprint, should stretch. But fitness walkers — those who spend at least twenty minutes at 60% to 90% of their maximum heart rates, a couple of times a week — and long-distance walkers definitely need to warm up and cool down.

Walking will not improve your flexibility in general. A lack of flexibility can set you up for injuries. Early on in my walking experience, I could easily touch my toes, but after a few months of walking, my calves and ankles were tighter than they had ever been before. The reason is that walking causes the muscles in the back of the legs to contract. Repeated contractions shorten these muscles, tendons, and ligaments. Stretching is the best way to prevent this.

Since walking is a low-impact exercise with a relatively small risk of injury, warm-ups can be simple and short. Of course, if you have some stiffness or a history of injury, you will want to spend a little more time limbering up. The key is to listen to your body.

There is nothing difficult about stretching for a walk, but like everything else there is a right way and a wrong way.

Stretching is a gradual process — you will not reach your maximum flexibility with one enormous stretch. Never bounce or lunge during a stretch since these are easy ways to strain or tear muscles!

! BREATHING

Many people forget to breathe when they stretch. Nothing could be worse. You will find that slow, rhythmical breathing will help you stretch even farther.

Breathing correctly also increases your oxygen transport capacity. This is the greatest amount of oxygen your body can move in a measure of time. As people age or fall ill to disease, they have to breathe harder and faster than our young healthy counterparts do to maintain the same aerobic performance. Furthermore, exercisers of all ages forget to breathe rhythmically as they are rapidly expending oxygen from their blood. That is why it is so essential to breathe. In doing so, you restore your body with its fuel, so breathe as often and as heavy as you like.

! DON'T OVERDO IT

All of our muscles have a built-in stretch reflex. When a muscle's nerve senses over-stretching, the muscle experiences an involuntary contraction, thus trying to avoid possible injury. Ironically, when you attempt to stretch too far, you actually tighten the very muscle you are trying to relax.

Holding a stretch beyond a muscle's current flexibility not only hurts, but also damages the muscle by tearing the microscopic muscle fibers. Just as a scar forms when you cut yourself, a muscle also scars when damaged. Ultimately, this reduces elasticity, and the muscle becomes tight and sore. Subsequently stretching becomes a dreaded experience when it should relax you and make you feel good.

Many of us have been misguided by the time-worn myth, "No pain, no gain." In stretching, nothing could be further from the truth. Proper stretching is not painful. Pain, in fact, should tell you something is wrong with your stretching technique or indicate a previously damaged muscle or tendon. In such cases, do not hesitate to see your doctor.

Most stretches should be held for thirty seconds and

then can be gradually increased to sixty seconds. A few last minute reminders:

1. Remember to breathe.
2. Don't overextend yourself — let up if you feel discomfort.
3. Perform two sets of each stretch position.
4. *Enjoy stretching.*

❗ *BEGINNING TO STRETCH*

To start, spend about thirty seconds and go to the point at which you feel a mild tension. Relax as you hold the stretch. As you hold the stretch, you should begin to feel the tension subside. If you find the degree of tension uncomfortable, ease off a bit until you find something that you can handle.

INTERMEDIATE STRETCH

Next, move just a little bit farther in your stretch until you again feel a mild tension and hold it for about thirty seconds. As you are holding the stretch and breathing, the tension should diminish. If not, ease off until the discomfort lessens.

❗ *UPPER BODY STRETCHES*

HEAD ROLLS

Assume a standing a position with your arms at your sides. Roll your head around your chest, shoulders, and back several times in both directions. Now flex your head forward by dropping your chin down as far as possible.

Then extend your head as far backward as possible. This exercise improves neck flexibility and also helps firm muscles in front of the neck. (See photos 7, 8, 9.)

STANDING STRETCH

This stretch is excellent for stretching the muscles from your side all along the arms to the hips. I refer to it as the *full body stretch.*

Stand with your feet together and toes pointed straight ahead. Place both hands overhead and clasp together. Now,

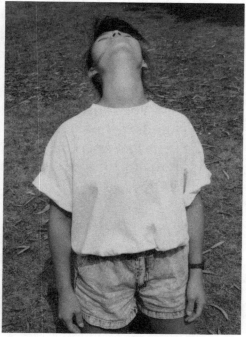

7. *Head rolls loosen ligaments and tendons in the lower chin, neck, and back.*

8. *This portion of the roll stretches the lower neck.*

9. *The human spine is the nerve center of the body. Full head rolls loosen the spine and help to release tension.*

as though you are reaching for something high above you, slowly bend to the right. (See photos 10, 11, 12.)

Form is critical in order to get maximum benefit from this stretch. The head should remain level and eyes should be focused straight ahead. Pick out an object in the room and don't let your eyes veer from it. Do two sets with both sides.

For those with weak backs, instead of extending both hands in the air, use one hand to support your hip and spread your feet apart slightly. Every other position and movement remains the same. Do two sets with both sides. (See photos 13, 14, 15.)

❗ LEG STRETCHES

LEGS, CALVES, AND ACHILLES TENDONS

These stretches will give you flexibility and bring energy to your legs.

To stretch the calf, stand a small distance from a wall or post and lean into it with your forearms. Bend one leg and place your foot on the ground in front of you, with the other leg extending straight behind you. Slowly move the hips forward, keeping your lower back flat. It is essential to keep the heel of the back leg firmly planted on the ground with the toes slightly turned as you hold the stretch. Do two sets. Repeat with the other leg. (See photo 16.)

To stretch the top of the foot and the shin, maintain the same position against the post, bend both knees, and dip your body downward. Keep the front foot flat on the ground while flexing the top of the back toe into the ground. Because the small muscle of the shin is rarely used, you may often feel tightness there while hill walking. (See photo 17.)

For the calf and Achilles tendon, lower the hips downward as you bend the knee slightly. The back remains flat. Your back foot should be slightly toed-in. Once again, the heel remains firmly planted on the ground. Be careful when stretching the Achilles tendon. It only needs a slight stretch. Do two sets. Repeat with other leg.

Another great stretch for the calf and Achilles tendon is the curb stretch. Supporting your body with a hand on a sign, back of a bench, etc., stand on the edge of the curb with one

10. *This stretch reaches nearly every part of the body. Done properly, it requires enormous concentration. Reach for the sky. Every part of your body should be flexed and tight. Contract every muscle, pick an object in the distance and do not veer from it.*

11. *Slowly bend to one side. Nothing bends and the eyes remain focused. Continue to reach for the clouds. Notice the muscles flexed around Christine's knees. This is a sign of discipline and intense concentration. This stretch is not easy, but the payoff is the enormous release of tension that is forced from your body.*

12. *And the final bend. Even Christine, a professional aerobicizer, has difficulty keeping her eyes focused. This stretch is very powerful. If you are interested in yoga, be prepared for stretches like these.*

13. *This stretch is the beginner/interme-diate side stretch. If you are unable to do the previous stretch, this is for you. Spread your feet a little more than shoulder width apart. Place one hand on your waist and reach for the sky with the other hand.*

14. *Slowly lean to the side.*

15. *Reach to the side until you feel moderate tension, and hold for ten seconds.*

16. *(Above) The calf stretch.*

17. *(At right) A great stretch for the shins, especially before and after walking hills.*

foot and slowly lower yourself until you feel moderate tension in the calf. Hold for ten seconds and repeat with the other foot. (See photo 18.)

QUADRICEPS AND HAMSTRING

Assume a bent-knee position with your heels flat on the ground, toes pointed straight ahead, and feet about shoulder-width apart. (See photo 19.)

In this position you are tightening the quadriceps and relaxing the hamstrings. As you hold this bent-knee position, feel the difference between the front of the thigh and the back of the thigh. The quadriceps (front) should feel hard and tight, while the hamstrings (back) should feel soft and relaxed.

HIPS, HAMSTRINGS, AND GROIN

To stretch the muscle in the front of the hip, from a kneeling position move one leg forward until the knee of the forward leg is directly over the ankle. Your other knee rests on the ground. Without changing the position of the knee on the

 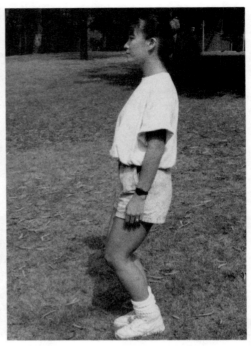

18. *The curb ankle stretch is an easy way to stretch the calf muscle and the Achilles tendon.*

19. *It looks almost useless, but this position will stretch the quadriceps very well.*

20. *To stretch the hamstring, move one leg forward until the knee of the forward leg is directly over the ankle.*

ground or the front foot, slowly lower the front of your hip downward. You should feel this stretch in the front of the hip and perhaps in the hamstrings and groin, depending on your current flexibility. (See photo 20.)

GROIN

Place the soles of your feet together and hold your toes. Gently pull yourself forward, bending from the hips, until you feel a little tension in your groin. Try to place your elbows on the outside of your legs and slowly bend the spine downward. Do not bounce. Do two sets. (See photos 21, 22.)

An alternative method, if you have trouble with balance, is to sit against a wall or couch, or with your back to your walking partner. With the back straight and the soles of your feet together, use your hands to push gently down on the inside of your knee. Push until you feel a little tension and hold. Do two sets. (See photo 23.)

QUADRICEPS

Sit with your left leg bent so that your left heel is just to the outside of your left hip. The right leg is straight out in front of you.

In this position your foot should be extended back with the ankle flexed. If your ankle is tight, move the foot just enough to the side to lessen the tension in your ankle.

Try not to let the foot flare out to the side in this position. By keeping your foot pointed straight back you remove the stress from the inside of your knee. The more the foot flares to the side, the more stress there is exerted on the knee. (See photos 24, 25, 26.)

Now, slowly lean straight back until you feel a mild tension. Use your hands for balance and support. Do not let the knee come up from the floor. This is an indication that you are over-stretching. Switch legs. Do two sets.

HAMSTRING

In a sitting position, straighten your left leg with the sole of your right foot slightly touching the inside of the left thigh. You are now in a straight-leg, bent-knee position. Slowly bend

22. *Bend as far to the ground as you can. This stretch will continue to stretch the groin to greater degrees. If you have not mastered the above stretch, defer this one until you are more flexible.*

21. *An easy stretch for the groin area. Please remember not to bounce the knees when pushing them down.*

23. *A tandem groin stretch. Until your partner's back feels like a wall, you are not in the correct position for this alternative groin stretch.*

24. *The sitting stretch for the quadriceps.*

25. *Lean backward slowly, supporting yourself with your hand. Do not exert yourself, as you could strain your back.*

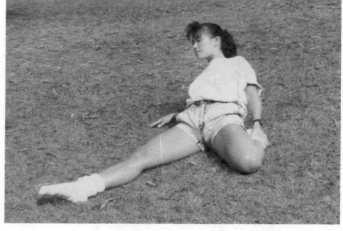

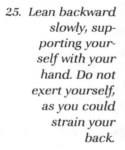

26. *Only for the most flexible and advanced athletes. Take it one step at a time.*

forward from the hips toward the foot of the straight leg until you feel tension. After the tension has diminished, bend a bit more and hold. (See photos 27, 28, 29, 30.)

During this stretch, keep the foot of the straight leg upright with the ankle and toes relaxed. Be sure that the quadriceps are relaxed during this stretch. If you cannot easily reach your feet, use a towel to help you stretch.

UPPER LEG

From a sitting position, with one leg extended straight out, slowly bring your bent knee as one unit to your chest. Pull it forward until you feel a gentle stretch in the back of the upper leg. You may want to do this stretch while you rest your back against a wall or the back of a couch. Hold for twenty seconds. (See photo 31.)

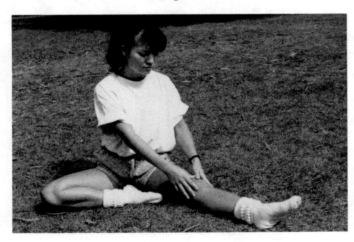

27. *The starting position for a hamstring stretch. Notice the position of the bent leg.*

28. *Slowly reach as far as you can. Deep breathing will help you extend your stretch incrementally. Go as far as you can and hold this position for twenty seconds.*

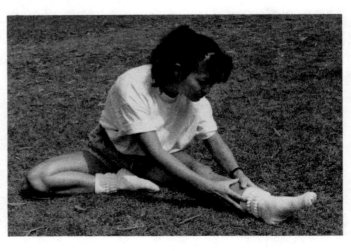

29. *A full stretch with the forehead on the knee is for the most flexible walker.*

30. *Use a towel to help you stretch if you cannot easily reach your feet. Men will most likely need a towel.*

31. *Pull your knee as one unit toward your chest, and hold the position for twenty seconds.*

! *ANKLE AND FOOT STRETCHES*

Our feet are precious. They bear the weight of our bodies for a lifetime, but they need some special attention. Here is a series of stretches that will leave your feet feeling wonderful.

Lie flat on your back and extend the toes as far as they will go. You should feel tension across the top of your feet. (See photo 32.)

While sitting up, rotate your ankles clockwise and counterclockwise through a complete circle of motion, providing slight resistance with your hand. This motion helps to stretch slightly tight ligaments and tendons. Repeat ten to twenty times in each direction.

Next, use your fingers to pull the toes gently toward you. This will stretch the top of the foot and the tendons of the toes. Now pull the toes in the opposite direction to stretch the top tendons of the foot. Hold each stretch for ten seconds and repeat three times. (See photos 33, 34, 35, 36, 37, 38.)

And finally, with the flat part of your fist, gently strike along the sole of the foot, moving from heel to toe in a vigorous motion. Repeat on the other foot.

Every human body is unique and may require some additional stretches. You know your body better than anyone else does. If you feel tightness somewhere, do what feels right — slowly and with no bouncing.

Your muscles need to wake up just as you do. A full stretching routine should be done before and after each walk. Neglecting a proper stretch and warm-up routine is a frequent cause of avoidable injury. Be smart.

32. *Does it look easy and relaxing? It is! Not only does this stretch the top of the foot, but it also doubles as a great wake-up stretch before you get out of bed. Just lay there and stretch all you want. It's a great way to start the day.*

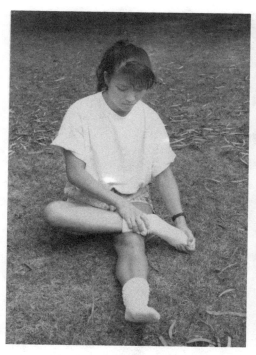 

33. Be kind to your feet. Grip the top of your toes with the opposite hand, secure your ankle with the other hand, and rotate your foot clockwise. It is very important to relax the ankle. Your body's natural reaction is to constrict the muscle.

34. Following through in a downward clockwise motion. Repeat with the other foot.

35. Remain seated with the ankle resting on the knee. Firmly grip all of the toes and pull them back. Continue to pull until you feel a lot of resistance, and hold for ten seconds.

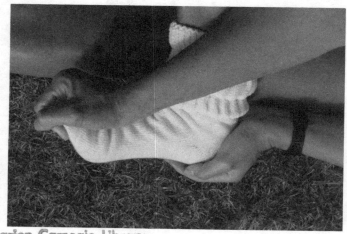

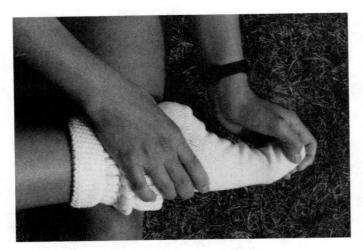

36. Now pull the toes forward in the opposite direction.

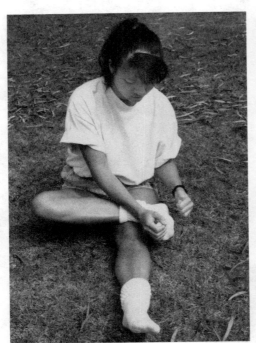

37. A wonderful conditioner to open and stimulate the blood vessels in the sole of the foot. Grip toes and pull them away from you. Now, with a vigorous motion, rapidly strike the sole of the foot, moving from heel to toe and back to the heel.

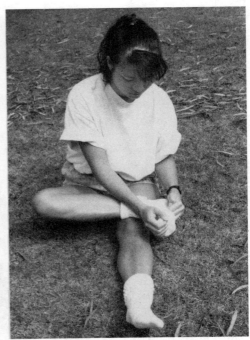

38. Repeat this exercise for twenty seconds on each foot, and you will feel like your feet are brand-new.

CHAPTER 4

Walking Equipment

. . . If one just keeps on walking, everything will be all right.
Kierkegaard

The beauty of walking is that it requires absolutely no equipment. Stark naked, you can step outside your door and begin walking. But our world is not quite so pure anymore, so walking equipment abounds, all of it designed to improve the comfort and quality of your walk. Although the general walking equipment described below follows a distant second behind the importance of walking shoes, once having tried some of the other items, you may wonder how you ever got along without them. Enjoy your shopping!

❗ WALKING APPAREL

Regardless of how cold the weather is, if you exercise, you perspire. Damp clothing turns cold, which removes vital body heat and reduces the insulating value of the rest of your clothes. Natural fibers such as cotton and wool absorb moisture but are extremely slow to dry. And the traditional rain slicker only adds to the problem by sealing the moisture in. You create steam that has nowhere to escape, and you begin to get the chills. (See photos 39 & 40 at top of next page.)

Enter the world of synthetic fibers. While maintaining the look and feel of cotton, they eliminate the problem of retained moisture. These fabrics wick away moisture and allow it to evaporate from your skin through the outer layers of your

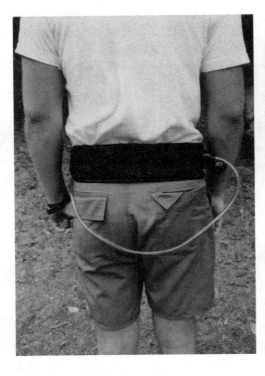

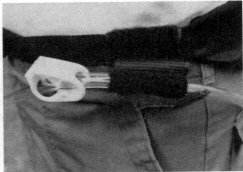

39. & 40. *This water bottle around the waist holds one quart. You'll never have to take time to search for a water fountain again. Drink from the tube for instant refreshment. The white clamp is a valve to turn on and off the flow of water.*

clothes. Today's breathable, waterproof outer garments keep the wet from getting in, yet allow water vapor to escape.

LAYERED DRESSING

The golden rule for dressing to walk is layers. No matter what you wear, by wearing layers you have the most options – from warm-up to cool-down. The best layering system begins with three parts: a base layer, an insulating layer, and an outer layer. It is preferable to have too much insulation on your body than too little. You can always remove a layer at a time until you feel comfortable.

Of course, the actual number of layers and the types of materials you wear are determined by the weather, where you live, and how long and hard you walk.

OUTERWEAR

Outerwear should be purchased for a specific walking climate. On a bright, sunny day nothing is better than a 100%

cotton T-shirt. But beware; never assume that the weather is going to cater to your walk. On extended walks, carry rain gear.

THERMAL UNDERWEAR

For colder climates, you will want your primary layer to be thermal underwear. Wear only cotton since it absorbs moisture best and will allow the secondary layer to wick away your perspiration, thus keeping you warm and dry.

FLEECEWEAR

Fleecewear is the middle layer. It serves as an insulator, while drawing moisture from the body. A sweat shirt made of synthetic fibers will work fine.

SHORTS

Shorts should be comfortable. And for comfort nothing beats cotton. Cotton Bermuda shorts are ideal. Shorts with many pockets are even better for toting snack foods, cash, keys, and identification.

TIGHTS

Some walkers prefer the snug, supportive feeling of biking shorts. Usually designed of a polypropylene fleece, biking shorts wick moisture from the skin to keep you dry. However, you forgo pockets and "acceptable" attire for some eating establishments with this type of clothing.

Long tights are an extended version of biking shorts with all the benefits extended down to your ankles, including a great guard against the wind.

GLOVES/MITTENS

For colder climates, mittens are warmer than gloves, but whichever you choose should have a wind-proof, waterproof shell with thick insulation.

HEADGEAR

For visibility and warmth, an appropriate hat is important. For warm, sunny weather, wearing a wide-brimmed, bright-colored hat is prudent. Stay away from visors since they

---

FOOTSTEPS

Beware of the coldest cities in America. You may want to find an indoor mall during this time of the year. But don't even think about staying home!

City	Mean Temperature
International Falls, MN	36.4
Duluth, MN	38.2
Caribou, ME	38.9
Marquette, MI	39.2
Sault Sainte Marie, MI	39.7
Fargo, ND	40.5
Williston, ND	40.8
Alamosa, CO	41.2
Bismarck, ND	41.3
St. Cloud, MN	41.4

(Source: NOAA, National Climatic Data Center)

---

don't shield the top of your head from the sun. Not only does direct sunlight on your head raise your body temperature, but your scalp can burn. For cooler climates, a wool knit cap is essential.

SOCKS

The three things to look for in a walking sock are fiber content, construction, and padding.

Fiber Content. Look for a sock made primarily of acrylic fiber. A combination of acrylic and cotton will absorb moisture by wicking moisture from the foot. Moisture on the foot turns to steam, heats up the foot, and causes blister formation. There should be a higher percentage of synthetic fiber than cotton in the sock, since synthetic fiber pulls moisture from the foot while cotton absorbs it.

Construction. The sock should have a natural foot formation when it's off the foot. This prevents bunching and movement of the sock when being worn with shoes. A basic tube sock has a tendency to rub against the skin and form blisters.

Padding. Cushioning should be built into the heel and toe box — at the tips and over the toes. Be cautious of socks with too much padding since this can alter the fit of your shoe. Suitable socks can be found at sporting goods stores of all kinds.

SPORT BRAS

Based on numerous conversations with women, it seems that many women do not think that walking requires a sport bra. But walking creates a similar breast movement to running — perhaps even more among fitness walkers with their vigorous arm swing. With new comfort features like hypoallergenic fabric, seamless cups, and wider shoulder straps, you don't have to forgo comfort for support.

❗ *SHOES*

A relatively new saying has developed in the walking community: "You wouldn't wear basketball shoes to run, so why would you wear running shoes to walk."

Contrary to the belief of many, walking is not slow running. The mechanics, the weight distribution, and the motion of walking are all different from those of running. A few years ago this sounded quite absurd. Anyone could have told you that all shoes were made for walking.

But now, indeed, we know better. The technical breakthroughs in walking shoes give the simple pleasure of walking a complex twist of engineering and terminology.

THE ANATOMY OF A SHOE

Collar. The opening of the shoe; the part of the upper that wraps around your ankle.

Dual-density. Like triple density, this refers to materials, such as rubber, of varying degrees of firmness in the sole. There are several reasons for varying densities: softer materials add cushioning, while firmer materials add durability and stability.

EVA. Ethylene vinyl acetate is a soft, lightweight material commonly used for cushioning the midsoles of walking shoes.

Heel counter. The firm cup at the back of the shoe that wraps around the heel and provides lateral (outside) and medial (inside) stability.

Heel cradle. A part of the footbed that encircles the base of the heel, adding stability and comfort.

Heel cup. See *heel counter.* Also refers to a device added to the inside of the shoe for extra cushioning and protection.

Heel cushion. Any feature of the midsole or footbed designed for shock absorption in the heel area.

Heel plug. An insert into the midsole or outsole under the heel of the foot, added for stability and cushioning.

Heel stabilizer. A motion-control device that keeps the rear of the foot steady.

Insole. The footbed, or what the foot rests on; usually a sock liner or insert.

Last. The mold on which the shoe is wrapped.

Midsole. The cushioning material between the insole and the bottom of the shoe.

Notched heel collar. A notch cut into the back of the collar to prevent irritation of the Achilles tendon.

Orthotic. A pre-shaped footbed made by a podiatrist from a cast of an individual's foot. Some manufacturers use this term to describe insoles that are designed to conform to the foot as the shoe is worn.

Outsole. The very bottom of the shoe and the surface that comes in contact with the ground. A flared outsole (sometimes called a flared midsole), typically found on running shoes, widens below the foot for added stability.

Saddle. The flap that goes over the top of the foot, near the laces, to add arch support and stability.

Shank. A piece of firm material that runs from the ball of the foot to the heel, between the insole and the midsole, for added arch support.

Sock liner. The top layer of an insole that is sometimes contoured, removable, or treated with anti-bacterial chemicals.

Upper. The part of the shoe that rises above the insole, generally made of leather, canvas, or nylon.

Wedge. The thicker part of the midsole that makes the heel higher than the ball of the foot.

SELECTING YOUR SHOES

Socks. Decide on what type and how many socks you are going to wear. I recommend wearing a silk liner with a thick outer synthetic sock for padding and absorption. However, if you choose to wear another sock configuration, wear these when fitting your walking shoes. It's academic — the more sock, the bigger the shoe size you'll need.

Toe Box. With the shoes laced, you should be able to move your toes around freely without any rubbing or resistance against the shoe itself.

Last. The last should conform to the shape of the feet. Because all feet are different, no one pair of shoes is going to feel perfect, but it should conform closely to your foot in shape and proportion.

Tread. Unlike running shoes, a walking shoe should lie flat on the surface without any air space under the shoe. The tread itself should be fairly smooth, but have enough traction so you can stop yourself in emergencies or while going down steep inclines. (See photo 41.)

Padding. Adequate padding should be found around the collar and under the tongue.

Linings. Breathable materials should line the shoe throughout. Look carefully for any protruding seams or shoddy craftsmanship that could lead to pressure on your foot. What seems like just a piece of nylon thread can feel like a thorn after four miles of walking.

Heel. The heel should be reinforced with extra padding and shock absorption.

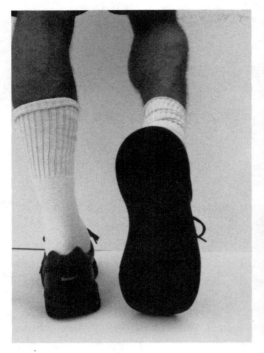

41. *Notice the thickness and flatness of the tread. This gives the walker a very solid, safe foundation with each step.*

42. *Notice the large toe box. Laces are a great place to hold keys and key holders securely.*

Weight. Lighter is better. However, do not sacrifice quality. Check to see if the shoe is well-made, then consider the weight. And if you like the look of walking boots for street wear, consider that you will be carrying that extra foot load with you every step of the way.

Width. Many shoe manufacturers offer shoe sizes with only a few width selections. For those with extra wide or narrow feet, you will want to consider a shoe that offers various width sizes.

Style. As always, style is a matter of personal taste.

CARING FOR YOUR SHOES

Dirt. Dirt is the ubiquitous destroyer of leather shoes. After each walk, take a damp cloth and wipe all the external dirt and dust off the shoes. Dry out the shoes, too, including the tongue.

Leather. If your shoes are constructed of leather, a leather cleaner and conditioner should be used periodically. The frequency of leather cleaning will be determined by how often you walk and the sort of terrain you walk in.

Also, when new shoes are putting pressure on your feet as the creases in the shoes begin to form, a daily application of water and leather conditioner or saddle soap will expedite this process of breaking in shoes to fit your feet just right.

Soles. Average to good walking soles will last about 400 miles. Prior to that time, however, Shoo Goo, a special rubber salve, can be used to stop holes from forming and prevent the heel from becoming detached from the outsole.

To give your walking shoes a second life, most shoes can be resoled at about a third of the cost of new shoes.

MODIFYING SHOES FOR GREATER FIT AND COMFORT

Extra padding and heel and arch supports can all be added to the shoe to increase your comfort and the shock absorption level of your shoes.

Because the human foot is imperfect just as we are, there are flaws in its development. Fortunately, thanks to modern medicine, most every flaw is correctable through a branch of medicine called podiatry. Similar to what an orthodontist does with teeth, a podiatrist tries to straighten out our foot flaws.

By using inserts, lifts, modified shoe construction, and even surgery, foot doctors, as they are known, can get us up on our feet in no time. However, it is far cheaper and more comfortable to do what you can yourself.

LACING

Lacing your shoes properly can also make an enormous difference in the comfort and fit of your shoes. For this reason, when shopping for shoes always lace the shoes yourself. As we said before, remember to bring your own pairs of socks (silk liners and outers) so you will get an accurate fitting. (See photo 42.)

Most shoes laced without any thought are tighter toward the toe box and become gradually looser toward the top of the foot. Try reversing this to remove the pressure from the blood vessels leading into the toes, since they are constantly flexing and need unimpeded blood circulation.

AIRING SHOES

When your shoes become damp or wet, never set them by a heater to dry. The best drying method is to set them outdoors in indirect sunlight and with the laces removed. After several hours, remove from the sunlight and sprinkle them with a small amount of baby powder or a commercial deodorizer.

If you are pressed for time, use a hair dryer at its lowest temperature setting. You need to avoid direct sunlight or a high hair dryer setting because direct and hot heat dries out the leather's natural oils and leads to cracking.

❕ BABY CARRIERS

Given their popularity, many of you have no doubt seen on the road baby carriers that are carried on the parent's back or stomach. Dozens of models are available in every shape and size. Comfort is a critical factor for both carrier and baby. There are a few things to consider before you make your purchase. Can the child be easily loaded and unloaded into the pack? Are strap adjustments easy to make? Can the carrier be used by both parents? Is the carrier easy to move and transport? Does it fit well or does it bounce? Does it give adequate support to the child's head and neck? Does it have storage for baby supplies? Is it washable? Front carriers can be tough on the back and shoulders; once a baby can hold up his head, a back carrier is probably superior. Two kinds to consider are Kelty Pak (P.O. Box 7048-A, St. Louis, MO 63177; 800/325-4121) and Snugli (12980 West Cedar Drive, Lakewood, CO 80228-1903; 303/989-2181).

ALL-TERRAIN BABY STROLLERS

These are built like Volvos and cost about the same. If the stroller you are looking at does not look like it could withstand a roll-over without baby being dumped onto the pavement, then keep looking. A word of warning — they aren't cheap. They start at about $200. If they are inexpensive, determine why. Look at the craftsmanship. Look at the nuts and bolts. Remember, if the unthinkable should happen as you are walking over a protruding tree root, you will need to be sure that your child will be protected.

To find an all-terrain stroller, go wherever conventional strollers are found. Better yet, find some people who own one and get their recommendation.

BACKPACKS AND EQUIPMENT CARRIERS

FANNY PACKS

Is it so warm out you don't need a jacket? You've walked this same area many times before. You will be back in no time, right? You'll need no lunch, no water, no gear. Nothing!

You may think a day or fanny pack is unnecessary, but you have to discover for yourself that being prepared is necessary. I suggest you be prepared for a walk of any length over an hour. You do not need 500 cubic inches of storage to tote your essentials, just someplace to stash some cash, a journal or pad of paper, an extra T-shirt and hand towel for dealing with perspiration, some natural, wholesome food loaded with energy, a pair of sunglasses, and whatever else you desire. (See photo 43.)

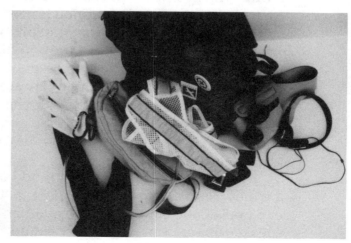

43. A buffet of walking equipment. Clockwise, from right to left: Backpack, Walkman™ and holder, sunglasses, reflector vest, fanny pack, waist water pack, and cotton gloves.

Fanny packs come in various sizes, colors, and dimensions. Check local sporting goods and outdoor stores. Prices begin at $20.

DAY PACKS

Some people, including myself, prefer the extra capacity and the feel of a backpack. If you want to carry a couple of extra pieces of clothing, a journal, a camera, and some food and water, you may be hard pressed to find room in a fanny pack. However, some walkers use two fanny packs, placed on opposite sides of their waist. Ultimately, the decision depends on your comfort. If you do choose a day pack, purchase one with a lot of pockets, made of canvas, and reinforced with a leather bottom. Day backs can be found at sporting goods and backpacking stores.

DOG PACKS

Absurd, you say? Why? He has four legs and you have only two. Why shouldn't Spot carry his own water and snacks? Try your local pet store or contact Eagle Creek (1665 South Rancho Santa Fe Road, San Marcos, CA 92069; 800/874-9925).

! CASSETTE PLAYERS

Listening to music or the news while walking helps pass the time, maintain your rhythm, and allay boredom during boring terrain. A player used sensibly is a great companion for your walk. However, a word of caution is needed here. Various new studies have determined that a combination of loud sound (especially with headphones) and aerobic exercise could lead to hearing loss or damage. To prevent irreparable damage to the ear, tune in only one hour a day at medium volume and even lower while exercising. If you ever hear ringing in your ear, stop listening immediately and seriously reconsider using your cassette player until you have consulted with your physician.

An alternative: If you don't mind being stared at once in a while, Toshiba offers a Sonic Jacket. The amplifier goes in one pocket, the battery pack in another, and four lightweight speakers in various compartments. You, of course, provide the cassette or compact disc player. At a hefty $200, it is an "audiophile-turned-walker's" dream. Contact Toshiba for more information (82 Totowa Road, Wayne, NJ 07470; 201/628-8000).

Or how about stereo sweats? With removable padded speakers in the hood, just connect your portable stereo with the pocket plug. The cost is $49.95 from Sport Electronics (P.O. Box 1412, Northbrook, IL 60062; 312/564-5775).

CASSETTE/COMPACT DISC CARRIERS

A portable cassette player will bounce a good deal when you are walking. Carrying it in your hand will inhibit an efficient, natural gait and arm swing. If you place the player in your pocket it has a tendency to mysteriously make its own adjustments as it bounces inside your pocket.

The best solution is to purchase a cassette carrier. Dozens of styles, colors, and fittings fill the marketplace. I find that a neoprene waist model with the player cradled just below the stomach fits snugly and does not interfere with my walking. (See photo 44.)

WALKING CASSETTE TAPES

There are a variety of fitness walking tapes on the market. Musical walking tapes are designed with your specific walking style and musical preferences in mind. There are tapes of the forties, fifties, and sixties, classical music, rock, jazz, new age, Latin, and much more. You will find pace tapes for strolling (three miles per hour) to race walking (six miles per hour). Most of the tapes are available through mail order. Look for the advertisements in the last few pages of *The Walking Magazine* (see glossary for address).

❗ FOOT CARE KIT

Ideally, every walker should carry a foot care kit. (See photo 45.) Prevention, as they say in medicine, is the best cure. The best prevention is to avoid developing a blister. However, when a blister, a toenail, or chafing begins to ruin a walk, some simple preparations make a great elixir. According to the mega-miler Robert Sweetgall, your kit should contain the following:

44. This little waist pack secures your cassette player on your body. You'll never have to worry about dropping it or holding it. Costs about $15.

1. rubbing alcohol and cotton balls to disinfect and clean the skin and syringe

2. iodine (disinfecting)

3. an insulin syringe to drain blisters

4. a bag of cornstarch to powder the feet

5. Bag Balm to lubricate the feet in colder weather

6. lanolin to moisturize the feet

7. collapsible scissors to trim toenails and shoes

8. single-edged razor for cuttings

9. moleskin for patching the feet and covering blisters (potential sore spots should also be covered with moleskin).

FIRST AID KIT

A basic first aid kit containing bandages (rubbing alcohol is in the foot care pack), a cortisone-based cream for insect bites, an Ace™ bandage, and a pain reliever such as Advil™ is recommended.

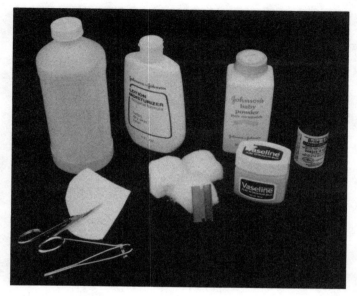

45. *Foot care kit. Clockwise from left to right: rubbing alcohol, lanolin, baby powder, iodine, Vaseline™, cotton, razor blade, nail clippers, moleskin, and scissors. Missing is a syringe.*

Perhaps the easiest thing to do would be to combine the foot care kit and the first aid kit rather than packing and caring two separate boxes.

❗ FOOT CARE ITEMS

There are a few other items that, while you probably won't want to carry them on your walks, will definitely help you and make you feel better when you arrive back home after a long walk.

Foot massager. There are many of these devices on the market. You probably already have everything you need without spending a large sum of money on these devices.

Toenail cutters are an absolute necessity in order to avoid ingrown toenails and a lot of pain. Toenails should be inspected daily, as should the feet.

Foot deodorants with antiperspirants prevent your feet from breathing. Do not use them. When you pull your feet out of a pair of shoes, it is the moisture in the shoe that smells. Dry out and deodorize your shoes and you will eliminate foot odor.

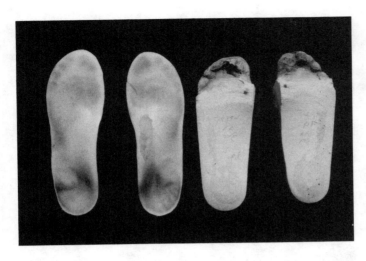

46. *My custom-made orthotics cost about $400 and are worth every cent.*

Orthotics. An orthotic is a corrective foot device inserted into the shoe. Orthotics differ from sole inserts because they are custom-made for the foot by making a plaster mold. They are formed to compensate for aberrations of the feet. (See photo 46.)

Sole inserts are store-bought devices used to give more support and comfort to the foot.

Insoles are the insert or sock lining on which the foot rests.

Heel cushions are a component of the foot bed that are designed to absorb and deflect shock away from the heel.

❢ MEASUREMENT DEVICES

Pulse monitors, fat calipers, blood pressure monitors, altimeters/barometers, stopwatches. For those who are strictly fitness walkers, knowing your changing body functions and overall progress is a must.

PEDOMETERS

A pedometer is a very handy device used for recording your mileage. By entering your average stride into its computer, it calculates the number of steps you take in feet. When you have walked 5,280 feet, you have walked a mile. Moreover, you have burned off at least one hundred calories.

The top-of-the-line pedometer will record your distance and steps taken, count the calories you have burned, keep track of walking time, sound a tone when personal, preset exercise goals are achieved, tell the time of day, and determine how much time remains in your walk with a countdown timer. Of course, there are also simpler models without all those read-outs. Prices for pedometers begin at about $15 and go up to about $40.

Call Sportline for a brochure containing their complete line (800/338-6337).

❢ MISCELLANEOUS EQUIPMENT

BINOCULARS AND CAMERAS

If you choose to explore the environment when you embark on a sensory walk, to really see things as you never have before, you may want to capture the moment with a camera or enhance the scene with a pair of binoculars.

COMPASS AND MAPS

If you are feeling adventurous and choose to walk off the beaten path, be smart and be prepared with a compass and a map of the area. To even the most experienced of explorers, a tree is a tree. In other words, do not rely on landmarks as your way out.

HAND WARMER

In extreme cold, or for those who get a case of cold hands in less-than-extreme temperatures, a disposable hand warmer is available in pocket size. This miniature furnace works with long-burning fuel sticks. For safety, the warming element is covered with velvet to prevent your hands from coming too close to the hot surface. For $2.50, these are a bargain for warm hands. Call mountaineering stores in your area to see if they carry them.

CHAPPED LIPS AND DRY HANDS

I'm sure you all know the wonders of ChapStick™. If not, reward yourself and buy some.

On long walks of five miles or more, you may notice that your hands become chapped, perhaps even visibly weathered. Due to the constant arm swing, your perspiration dries very quickly. After a while, layers of sweat will build up on your hand. If you doubt this, lick your palm the next time you are on a long walk. I will bet your hand tastes like table salt! If the dryness bothers you, as it does me, carry a small tube of lotion. Lanolin lotion is best.

WALKING STICKS AND STAFFS

A walking stick improves your balance, makes your stride more efficient, and helps you to build upper body strength. A walking stick in effect connects your upper body to the ground, allowing the large muscles in your arms to add power to your stride. This extra power is especially beneficial on steep hills. Try this experiment at home. Stand on a bathroom scale and push down on the floor with a broomstick. Notice how your weight falls. Determined by your weight, this translates into thousands of pounds being shifted to your upper body every mile.

In addition, a stick is a great scare tactic you can use against an over-zealous dog. A few companies with good walking sticks are: House of Canes and Walking Sticks (818/451-0745); Stan Novak Co. (800/443-7410); Ukay Inc. (513/779-2211); and Genuine Montana (800/553-4684).

DOG LEASH

Ideal for walking with your old buddy, dog leashes are available at pet shops. The good leashes extend up to about thirty feet and retract as you and your pet get closer to each other. With a push button brake so that you are always in control, these leashes range from $18 to $30, depending on length. Contact your pet supply store.

❗ REFLECTIVE/SAFETY EQUIPMENT

This includes reflective belts and trim, flashing reflectors, reflective bands and tape, and reflective vests. Whether you are an owl or a lark, or if you are walking anywhere with vehicular traffic, you need to be visible. Ideally, you should always dress in brighter colors to increase your visibility. However, total darkness requires some additional visibility enhancers. Usually a vest and some ankle bands will be sufficient. However, if you are wearing a backpack, you should wear belt or ankle reflectors with some reflective tape placed on your backpack.

❗ TREADMILLS

A treadmill simulates the activity of walking (or running) by moving the ground under you as opposed to you moving over the ground. There are two key features of owning these expensive aerobic machines. First, you can walk at precise and accurately measured speeds. This is important to anyone who wants to monitor each workout carefully. The second reason is that the intensity of your workout can be adjusted by adjusting the incline of the treadmill's running bed.

There are both motorized and non-motorized beds. The more accessories you want, the more you pay. Prices range from $600 for a manual treadmill to over $7,000 for the top-of-the-line electric version. Contact Precor for more information (P.O. Box 3004, Bothell, WA 98041-3004; 800/662-0606).

CHAPTER 5

Types of Walking and Their Benefits

You see differently when you walk.
Tony Converse, Producer

❗ *BEACH WALKING/BAREFOOT WALKING*

For most people, barefoot walking is nearly synonymous with beach walking. Beach walking also tends to be a somewhat seasonal exercise unless you live in a warm climate or dress appropriately for cooler weather.

Practice barefoot walking as much as you can. It strengthens your arches and toes, toughens the bottom of the feet, and gives them a rare opportunity to breathe. Walk barefoot around the house and in the garden during warm months. If you are concerned about stepping on something sharp, exercise sandals (available at sporting goods stores) with arch support are the next best thing. Try to avoid flat sandals since their surface does not support the natural arch of your foot.

Many athletes purposely train on sand more than any other surface because it allows the feet to achieve their full flexing motion as well as stretching leg muscles.

A normal walking speed for the beach is considerably slower than the standard three mile per hour. Indeed, you will be working hard at two miles per hour, but due to an increased heart rate you will reap exceptional cardiovascular benefits. If you have a competitive interest in walking or race walking, try working out daily in the sand. To maintain a rapid pace for a longer period of time, walk closer to the tide line. As your strength improves, you can use the various ranges of sand between the tide line and the dry sand to build upon your strength gradually. Despite the exhausting workout, barefoot walking may be sustained for longer periods without foot fatigue or blistering because there is no sock or shoe friction.

❗ NIGHT WALKING

It is always safer to walk during the day, but it can be a problem to do so with fewer daylight hours during the winter months. If you find night walking most suitable for you and your schedule, here are some special guidelines.

1. Wear bright clothing such as a white or yellow jacket or sweat shirt.

2. Use a reflective vest and ankle tape.

3. Stay on main thoroughfares and away from dark alleys or poorly lighted streets.

4. Leave a note at home indicating your specific route and when you anticipate returning.

5. As always, carry identification, a small amount of cash, grazing foods, and extra clothing.

❗ WALKING IN THE SNOW

Heavy snow walking has a training effect similar to walking in sand. With waterproof boots you can hike in packed snow, but unpacked snow will require snowshoes. Without them, walking (pronounced "trudging") through unpacked powder is trying indeed. Provided you are able to sustain a pace of any kind, snow walking will help intensify the resistance of your walking, thereby creating a greater metabolic benefit. In other words, by making walking more strenuous, you are giving yourself a better workout.

SNOWSHOES

Snowshoeing is the winter equivalent of hiking. Snowshoes allow the walker to stay on top of the snow and, with practice, "shuffle" across flatlands and climb up and down hills. Although the snowshoes greatly reduce the resistance that deep snow creates for the walker, it does force the walker to expend a great deal of energy while traveling over long distances, which ultimately burns more calories.

! POOL WALKING

Like weighted walking and pole walking (see the later section on Exerstriders), walking in a pool increases your energy expenditure. At one time or another, virtually everyone has attempted walking in the shallow end of a pool for a short period.

And just as with any other type of walking, speed determines your ultimate expenditure of energy and, ultimately, spent calories. The greater the limb movement against the resistance of the water, the greater the benefit will be.

Unfortunately, this type of walking requires a long time in the pool. Assuming you want to burn about 230 calories, it would take approximately an hour and a half at three miles per hour to do so. Both boredom and your skin's reaction to such a length spent in water should be considered before considering pool walking a part of your regular fitness routine.

Pool walking is best suited for patients who are recovering from leg or chest surgery, and thus cannot travel far and need control of their resistance factor. Note: Anyone recovering from surgery should have both his doctor's approval and constant pool-side supervision prior to pool walking.

! RACE WALKING

Race walking is to walking what running is to jogging. The main difference between walking fast and race walking is that in race walking the front leg must be fully locked at the knee in the support phase of the stride. Race walkers must pay more attention to their arm swing action than do non-race walkers, since their hands never reach higher or farther back than the chest. Race walkers stride as long as possible by rotating the hips forward and down as they move forward. By training and applying special techniques, they move at about twice the speed of the average fast walker.

Race walking, like walking, is growing rapidly. It is, as Dr. Sheehan says in his book, *Dr. Sheehan on Running,* "the perfect sport for recuperating from other sports . . . the ailing athlete who turns to race walking will soon find himself on the mend."

The rapid growth of race walking as a sport is even more pronounced considering that it is perceived as odd by the public. However, such odd movement is becoming hardly noticeable because new techniques control the inefficient and awkward-looking side-to-side movement of the hips. Think of your initial perception to the heavyhands™ movement (walkers carrying weights in their hands as they walked) or to martial artists (karate, judo, aikido) screaming and throwing legs and arms in the air. These activities appeared ridiculous until we began to understand them and their purpose. Initially, many race walkers are concerned about how they appear to others — the embarrassment factor — but once they learn the movements, these preoccupations disappear.

Race walking is so specialized that it would require a separate book to do it complete justice. Race walkers in top physical shape are some of the finest athletes, and many of the best are beyond the age of forty — indeed, an uncommon age to be at the top of one's game. In fact, many runners have turned to race walking because it not only improves their opportunities for qualifying competitions, but also reduces the running injuries that often force them to give up the sport altogether.

Actually, the race walking technique is similar to running, except that both feet never leave the ground at the same time. The race walker's gait is like that of the runner's in that there is a slight overlap of the feet. Training for race walking competition actually tends to be more grueling than preparing for a running competition. Race walkers build up their weekly mileage from 40 to more than 120 miles in an eight-week period. Moreover, many of their workouts are done at an exhausting five mile-per-hour pace or faster.

Race walking may not be for every walker. Nevertheless, the race walking technique has contributed to the overall efficiency and understanding of basic walking. Like a sculpted motorcycle clay prototype, early race walkers tried and tested every walking technique to determine which ones were best suited to economize their movement and speed. As more attention focuses on race walking, more techniques and improvements will doubtless evolve that will be applied to all forms of walking.

❢ ENDURANCE/LONG DISTANCE WALKING

Endurance walking is the marathon of the walker's world.

Suppose you are walking six miles a day. Multiply that by four and a half times, and you have a walking marathon. Multiply that by four and you have a feat few have matched in a single day — about one hundred miles. Walk across whole states. Walk across the entire country. This is endurance walking.

Most long-distance walkers, if their walks have been of heroic proportion, draw public attention as well as the public's affection. But no one has ever managed to do both for such a length of time as Edward Payson Weston.

Edward Payson Weston could easily walk one hundred miles in a day. But Weston did more than just race. He walked across America, talking on street corners, in churches, and at town squares, lecturing the masses on the values of walking and his experiences. He brought a new walking awareness to the masses. He became an American folk hero.

It is estimated that in his lifetime Edward Weston walked a distance equal to that of walking three times around the world — about seventy-five thousand miles! During a 3,500 mile walk from Los Angeles to New York, Weston, in a blizzard, crawled for many miles on all fours, using railroad tracks to keep himself on course. At the time he was seventy years old.

Aside from fame and an exhausting feat, there are many benefits to intrastate or intra-continental walks of endurance. Simply imagine what you might see in your own community when you walk — new restaurants, a new park bench on which to read a book, or an ideal spot to view the sunset.

When walking across the country you see everything — communities, cities, states, back roads, lifestyles, variations in climate and culture, a variety of animals and geography, and so much more — in microscopic detail. When walking free of fatigue (especially blisters and soreness), one begins to see the country in a different light. Free of societal confines, a sense of freedom overcomes the back road journeyman.

MY OWN EXPERIENCE

I well recall my own experience while walking round-trip from Los Angeles to San Diego — a distance of 240 miles. For my first endurance walk, it proved to be the best way to see the southern coast of California and experience the feeling of my feet moving forward for forty miles at a time. Despite twelve blisters and some leg cramps, I saw the coast as I never had and as only a walker could. There were periods in the wee hours of the morning when I shared the road with the occasional eighteen-wheeler gusting backdraft into my face. During my journey, I felt truly a part of the earth and not a mere inhabitant of it. Walking alone in desolate territory forces self-discipline; the mind wanders aimlessly, but sometimes with absolute purpose.

At any rate, I was not out to shatter any records; only to see if I could do it. It was my outlandish personal goal that came with many unexpected rewards. If one is in good physical shape and mentally prepared, it's uniquely rewarding.

ROBERT SWEETGALL

Currently, Robert Sweetgall is the most well-known long-distance walker in America. In September of 1984, sponsored by Rockport Corporation, he began a walking journey of the entire country that took 384 days, covered 11,208 miles, and took twenty million footsteps to accomplish. Rockport's mission was to record the effect that endurance walking has on the human body. Sweetgall's mission was and still remains to tell the world to take care of yourself and that walking is a great way to do that. He chronicled his journey in *The Walker's Journals*, in which he writes:

> None of us need to be great athletes to walk for wellness. You, me, everyone — we can all walk across America and discover the beauty that lies right in our own backyards. It's there waiting. Yet in our trendy way, we have turned "fitness" into a big business — fancy health clubs and all that shiny chrome. Yet you can get fit walking in fresh air for free . . .
>
> The jogging boom of the 70s inspired some, but did little for the many who needed inspiration the most. It gave . . . [many] the perfect excuse not to exercise. Why pound your body into destruction? Is it worth it? Is it enjoyable? Did you

ever see a jogger smile? For ten years I got caught up in the jogging craze my fitness perspective became so narrow — like how fast I could run a marathon.

More important than short-term fitness is long-term wellness. We've been brainwashed about body weight, body fat, and body muscle. Health clubs are full of muscle building equipment. Yet did you know anyone who died from lack of strength. So many people exercise for all the wrong reasons. To be fit is good, but it's only a temporary state. A week of bad habits, and your fitness is gone. To achieve it you make a commitment for life. How many 75 year old weight lifters and aerobic dancers do you know. Walking is the one exercise that will last you a lifetime. And to all those who complain, 'Walking takes too much time,' I ask, 'What's your hurry, and where are you going?'

COMMUTING/CITY WALKING

Depending on what city you live in, walking may be the best way to get where you are going. Sometimes a combination of driving your own vehicle, using public transportation, and walking the final leg to your destination is the most practical mode of getting from point A to point B.

Of course, some cities are more conducive to walking to and from work than others. I have lived in both Los Angeles and San Francisco. In Los Angeles it would be enormously impractical for many people to walk between home and their workplace. The geography is such that many of L.A.'s business and residential sectors are isolated from each other by an average thirty-minute commute in the car! Walking that distance alone is not entirely unrealistic, but considering air quality, traffic congestion, and the lack of walking-friendly areas, Los Angeles can be summarily dismissed as a realistic commute-by-walking metropolis.

San Francisco, however, could not have been more intelligently designed for the pedestrian. Not only does fast, clean, and timely public transportation abound, but the air quality and inherent beauty of the city make for an enjoyable walk, even when commuting to work. (See photo 47.)

Most cities fall somewhere in between in their "walkability." Many range between the impracticality of pedestrian commuting in Los Angeles to the ideal walking geography of San Francisco.

47. *San Francisco lunch hour. Walking, walking everywhere!*

On days when you do walk to work, plan ahead and have some clean clothes and toiletries with you or at the workplace so you can shower or freshen up before the day begins. Depending on the route(s) you take, you may discover a wonderful pastry shop along the way so you can integrate a healthy breakfast into your walk.

Pedestrian commuting is an ideal way to avoid the traffic rush hour and looking for a parking place. Best of all, you are giving your body one of the best aerobic workouts there is, and if you enjoy it, then what a wonderful discovery you have made — you are getting your exercise on your way to work!

And to those of you living in Los Angeles, try biking!

❢ EXPLORING A NEW CITY

You can know a city well only by walking it. When I was relocating to San Francisco, I happily left my car in Los Angeles and purchased a comfortable pair of walking shoes, because I knew that the only logical way I could move about and come to know the city was by walking the streets.

I can never understand people's willingness, upon encountering a new city, to rent a car or go below ground to take the subway, when they could take off on their own power at any time for free. Walking the streets and back alleys of a metropolis is a fascinating experience.

Walking while people-watching is a sure way to get to know the rhythm of the city. I was overwhelmed by the extreme human diversity I saw during walks in my city — the homeless, punks, posers, executives, shopkeepers, Chinese, gay, straight, young, old, Hispanic, Japanese, etc. I found that to come to know and understand the rhythm of a new city, you have to throw yourself into a mood and an energy of loving humanity and walk the streets.

You, the walker, are free to walk all you want. Free to walk in and around a traffic snarl and be on your way as drivers blow their horns while cursing in single syllables. The lazy driver is confined to the road, but the walker has no commitment other than to watch out for possible hazards.

Every city has a story to tell. While exploring San Francisco, I have begun piecing together her history. Inevitably, there are chapters missing. Curiosity to learn about these missing pieces can lead you to research the past and see old black and white photos chronicling buildings destroyed, earthquakes, and natural disasters that have been cosmetically sealed by mortar, concrete, and asphalt.

Both challenge and joy exist in the walker's ability to find the missing pieces of the puzzle — to recreate what has long since been consumed by the jaws of history. The mystery awaits. Go discover it!

❗ HIGH ALTITUDE WALKING

High altitude adds a new dimension to walking. Unlike walks at or near sea level, a mountain ascent has an ultimate final destination. And with the growing number of walking tours offered, destinations that were once the exclusive domain of expert mountaineers are now accessible to large numbers of walkers eager to explore the back roads.

However, a word of caution. About a quarter of those who travel above 8,000 feet experience AMS, or Acute Mountain Sickness. The symptoms include headache, listlessness, shortness of breath, nausea, impaired appetite, insomnia, and loss of coordination. Symptoms vary from mild irritation to extreme pain. Unheeded, AMS can lead to pulmonary edema and/or cerebral edema – potentially fatal conditions.

Some of the the factors contributing to this impairment are less oxygen, lower air pressure, and lower temperature. Meanwhile, the effects of gravity increase the strain on the body. The increased energy expended, coupled with less oxygen, leads to the most common symptom of AMS, shortness of breath.

At higher elevations the body needs a chance to adapt to the lower pressure and thinner air, so be careful not to walk or hike more than a 1,000-foot ascent per day.

Dehydration creates more problems. Within a two-week period, your body can make adjustments to compensate for the higher elevations. It does this by requiring a greater-than-usual need for water, which is due to a higher breathing rate and increased perspiration. You should always have water on hand — one to two gallons between meals should be anticipated, depending on your weight.

PREPARATION

You can train for high altitude walking by strengthening your heart and increasing your oxygen intake capacity. You won't achieve this through slow or moderate walking. The quickest way to increase your blood flow and breathing rate is to walk hills. Your goal is to increase your heart rate to about 80% of its potential. You may feel discomfort in the back of your calves and you may have some exerted breathing, but keep going. You will notice improvement if you just stick with it.

ACCLIMATE YOUR BODY

As your body ascends the mountain and travels through various layers of the atmosphere, it needs time to adjust to the lower pressure and thinner air. Generally, if your ascent within a twenty-four hour period extends beyond 1,000 feet, you may experience a number of AMS side effects. If they persist, descend 2,000-3,000 feet.

❗ *WEIGHTED WALKING*

Unfortunately, many people walk almost solely for fitness. And like most fitness programs catering to time-poor professionals, the goal is to pack as much weight loss and/or muscle toning into the shortest period of time as is possible. (See photos 48, 49, 50.)

In doing so, the fitness professional must consider the three primary elements on which all exercise depends: fre-

48. *Use side-to-side motion with hand weights. Studies have shown that over time some walkers could injure their muscles and ligaments and raise their blood pressure by using these walking devices.*

49. *Walkers/aerobicisers have a tendency to forget about form. Notice the hands being thrown from side to side. Shoulder muscles have to counter the outward momentum each time to bring the arm through its complete cycle.*

50. *Does it look fun?*

quency, duration (the length of time spent exercising), and intensity (metabolic expenditure) of the fitness activity.

In the tradition of supply and demand, fitness-walking innovators have capsulized the fitness benefit of walking into the least amount of time. Carrying hand weights (or wrist and ankle weights) boosts the oxygen and calories expended while walking by increasing the *intensity* of the workout.

However, the risks outweigh the benefits. When weights are added to the ends of the extremities, the muscles and connective tissue must work to move the weight first in one direction, then overcome the momentum and move in the opposite direction.

Although the muscles can usually bear the continuous strain, the connective tissues, which are not designed to bear such resistance, are typically over-stressed and may incur substantial damage in some cases.

In addition, carrying weights while walking elevates the blood pressure disproportionately to one's body weight. Those who enter any physical activity should be concerned about high blood pressure, particularly if they have not exercised for a while.

! *EXERSTRIDER*™

The Exerstrider™ consists of a pair of walking sticks that resemble cross-country ski poles with rubber pegs. Exerstriding, as it is called (the technique of walking, jogging, or bounding while using Exerstriders), offers all the increased intensity benefits derived from weighted walking without sacrificing the natural walking gait or risking the higher incidence of injury. (See photos 51, 52.)

The poles, which weigh less than a pound, are tailored to your height. The purpose of using the Exerstrider in lieu of regular "walking" is to increase your metabolic rate. You consume 20% to 50% more oxygen calories. In addition, you will increase your muscle mass in the upper body — something that walking alone does not do very well. And because with each step you are pushing off with the poles, you are simultaneously reducing the stress placed on your knee and hip joints. You are also contracting your upper body muscles thousands of times a mile against the resistance generated by pushing off with the Exerstrider. To illustrate, stand tall and

51. *Taking on a hill with the help of Exerstriders™.*

52. *Exerstriders™ are designed to work the upper body and take weight off your feet with each step.*

push down with both hands on the countertop in the kitchen. Do you feel your abdomen, triceps, and biceps contracting? This is what happens thousands and thousands of times as you "Exerstride."

And it is safe! Exerstriding is to weighted walking what bench pressing 150 pounds (my weight) is to doing push-ups. Exerstriding remains true to walking's simplicity by removing so little of its essence. And as far as arm swing, a drill sergeant could not give you better form. With Exerstrider it is difficult to cross your arm swing, raise your arms too high, or bring them too low. Your posture is greatly improved as well. In fact, I have recommended use of the Exerstrider to a caretaker for her elderly patient to use. They are lighter and stronger than a cane, and two are better the one. Perhaps, a "Rehabilastrider" could be developed with sturdier foot pegs and some more appropriate markings.

Perhaps the biggest obstacle to overcome is embarrassment. I concede that my first Exerstriding workouts began at 4 A.M. — a bit larkish even for me! However, as skateboards, in-line roller skates, and heavyhands™ have been met with acceptance through extensive use, so too will Exerstriders.

CHAPTER 6

Walking versus Other Exercise

Walking briskly, not just strolling, is the simplest and also one of the best exercises.
American Heart Association

Of the ten leading causes of death in the United States, nine are related to human lifestyles. If you have a sedentary lifestyle, your body's ability to function declines. If this deterioration persists, you place stress on your organ systems.

The good news is that you can do something about it. Moderate amounts of exercise can help you look and feel better, and enjoy life more. Indeed, your life will take on new meaning when you feel physically fit.

❗ AEROBIC EXERCISE

We are all aerobic organisms. Exercises referred to as "aerobic" require large amounts of oxygen. Oxygen is brought into your body with the air you inhale. Lifestyle behaviors that impair your respiratory or circulatory system, such as smoking or not getting enough exercise, reduce your ability to produce the life-sustaining oxygen your body needs. This decline in oxygen delivery is analogous to a slow form of suffocation, which makes you feel tired and sluggish. If this deterioration continues, eventually you will only be able to take in enough oxygen to sustain your life in a near state of rest.

Because human beings are aerobic organisms, exercise

improves our ability to use oxygen efficiently. Thus, walking stimulates the oxygen delivery system by using large muscle groups in a rhythmic and continuous manner.

UNDERSTANDING AEROBIC AND ANAEROBIC

Our bodies have two ways to create energy. One method is with oxygen (aerobic) and the other creates energy in the absence of oxygen (anaerobic).

Anaerobic exercise uses oxygen for small periods of time — usually just a few minutes. The hundred-yard dash or bench pressing 150 pounds are anaerobic activities. Anaerobic activities use small bursts of energy. Lifting weights and using Nautilus or Cybex equipment at the gym, as I once did, are not useless. Adequate body strength complements overall fitness. But consider how many people you have known who died due to inadequate physical strength.

Aerobic exercise produces 90% of the body's needed oxygen both in exercise and at rest. "Aerobics," as it is now called, is a series of exercises that require a maximum amount of oxygen.

❗ WALKING AND WEIGHT LOSS: AN IDEAL COMBINATION

Walking can expend lots of calories. Like in most aerobic activities, large muscle groups of your body, such as the quadriceps, are used for relatively long periods of time. In fact, walking a mile burns about the same number of calories as jogging does per mile (one hundred calories). Some argue that walking takes longer. However, this may be a welcome change from the breakneck speeds at which many Americans live their daily lives.

Sustained aerobic exercise plays a wonderful trick on your body. As you build up fat-burning cells (muscle), you reduce the size of the fat-storing cells, which to our chagrin reside in our pot bellies, love handles, and fat dimples. But because you can walk a longer amount of time than you can do just about any other aerobic activity, you are able to eliminate more calories (and therefore fat cells) without the exhaustion, stress, and fatigue inherent in running.

And as you're losing weight, walking stimulates your sense of well-being by reducing stress and tension. The temptation to cheat on a diet is highest during bouts with tension and anxiety. After a hectic day, you are most apt to indulge in food or drink. Walking, however, quells your appetite and reduces idle snacking time, while improving your mood.

❢ WALKING VERSUS RUNNING

The jogging craze of the 1970s gave all the couch potatoes the perfect excuse not to exercise. Alas, jogging was perceived as a strenuous exercise.

There is no question that jogging can be pleasurable, but too often there is pain mixed with the pleasure. Jogger's Ankle (sprains accounting for three-quarters of joggers' ankle injuries) has become a feared term and is commonplace in orthopedic offices. Since our feet contain one-fourth (twenty-six) of our body's bones, as well as muscle ligaments and yards of blood vessels, many doctors, understandably, favor brisk walking in lieu of jogging for achieving and maintaining physical fitness for a lifetime. Indeed, as walking is virtually risk-free, the oldest exercise continues to be the safest.

It would be untrue to say that James Fixx, the running guru of the 1970s and '80s, died due to running. It is rather ironic now that running can be viewed as an exercise rife with potential problems for runners.

First, consider that running pounds the joints relentlessly mile after mile at three times the impact of walking. Assume you weigh 150 pounds. That means that every time your leg strikes the ground, you are creating a 450-pound impact that is absorbed by your entire body — joints, ankles, hips, and back. It is no wonder, then, that running maintains one of the highest incidences of ankle, knee, hip, and back injuries of any sport.

To begin a running program that is as safe, easy, and effective as one hour of walking requires careful conditioning; you actually need to get in shape before you can begin getting into shape. Unless you are among the few who are skeletally and biomechanically suited for running, it is unlikely that you will stick with your exercise for more than a few weeks. And only the exercise that you are going to do for the rest of your life will keep you fit the rest of your life.

Try to recall the last time you saw someone running. Was that person breezing along with a refreshed, happy face? Probably not. More likely, you saw a contorted face staring obliviously into the distance — while you, the walker, move along at your own pace, capable of completing many more pleasant miles as the runner is recuperating from his pounding workout.

JOGGER INJURIES

When joggers jog, they land with approximately three times their body weight. Each time they leap up in the air, the impact is increased to between three and five times their body weight. Furthermore, as runners enter their forties and fifties, they want to remain fit, but the likelihood of experiencing knee, back, and ankle injuries increases rapidly. While walking, you always have one foot on the ground and land with only one and one-half times your body weight. This reduces the stress placed on the joints and decreases the possibility of a serious injury.

FOOTSTEPS

Don't Jar Your Joints

- Wear good walking shoes. There is no substitute for the support and shock absorption they provide. Make sure they fit well, with enough room to turn your toes under in the toe box.

- Warm up before you walk. Ten minutes of stretching will make your walk safer and more enjoyable. Don't take short cuts, or you will feel it later when you walk.

- Cool down after you walk. Five minutes of stretching while your body is warm will make your next walk all the easier.

- Stay lean. Watch your diet. How many overweight ninety-year-olds do you see walking around?

- Your body knows best. Listen to it. If it tells you to stop, then *stop!* Or make some modifications until it is happy again.

JAMES FIXX'S LEGACY

The tragic death of James Fixx, the guru of the running movement in the mid-1980s, left the world with an ironic situation. Although he had previously been in poor health (before changing his ways, he had a heart condition, was overweight, and smoked heavily), running did not cause Fixx's death. Nevertheless, it did lead exercisers to believe that running was not the only path to a healthy existence.

One man by the name of Robert Sweetgall walked across the U.S. to prove it. In 384 days Robert Sweetgall walked 11,208 miles across America. He asks, "Why pound the body into destruction? Is it really enjoyable? Do you ever see joggers smile? How many seventy-five-year-old joggers do you know?" Indeed, walking is the one exercise that will last you a lifetime.

❗ WALKING VERSUS OTHER SPORTS

SWIMMING

Swimming is good for building upper body strength, but it does not work for the legs very well. Swimming does nothing to build the skeletal system because it is not weight bearing. If you do not have a pool in your backyard, you also must consider the commute required and the size of the pool available. If you are a swimmer, that is great. Keep it up. Swimming is a great conditioner in its own right and makes a wonderful addition to walking.

BICYCLING

Bicycles are machines that do most of our work for us. You must choose to pedal hard enough to keep your pulse rate steady for a period of forty-five minutes to obtain a sustained aerobic benefit. To do this, you will have to travel a long way and, like swimming, bicycling is non-weight bearing. In addition, a bike can be quite costly, and there is always a chance of theft when leaving it unattended for even a moment. Finally, bikes are vehicles that must follow the rules of the road. Being careless on your bicycle is dangerous. I have witnessed many bicycle accidents while walking — many of which have been due to neglect on the cyclist's part. Be careful. Or walk, instead!

FOOTSTEPS

Ahh . . . Those Calories . . .

Activity	Calories Burned in 1 Hour
Walking (4 mph)	348
Uphill Walking (4 mph, 10% upgrade)	683
Running (6 mph)	727
Running (8 mph)	946
LifeCycle (Level 4, Hills)	480
Cross-Country Skiing	450
Tennis (singles)	420
Swimming (.5 mph)	300

(City Sports, August 1991)

ROWING

This is an outstanding aerobic exercise, but unless you have a body of water and a boat, you are limited to using a rowing machine. This is an expensive and, in my view, a boring form of exercise. However, it is a great aerobic adjunct to walking.

COURT SPORTS

Tennis, racketball, handball, and volleyball are competitive and exciting sports and can be good exercise as long as you choose to play long and hard. The obvious disadvantage is that there is continuous stop-and-go action that prevents you from obtaining a sustained aerobic benefit. Moreover, court games require commuting to facilities, gathering equipment, and finding equally skilled opponents with whom to compete.

ROLLER SKATING

Roller skating has recently been replaced by roller blading. Roller blading is an excellent aerobic activity provided you skate on a smooth, clean surface and have a lot of visibility, since your stopping power is quite poor. Some do view the new sport as dangerous, so be careful. When skating on sidewalks, be especially careful of buckled portions of concrete often caused by tree roots extending under the sidewalk.

TEAM SPORTS

Football, softball, bowling, etc., are great fun, but far too much time is spent waiting for something to happen. Although these sports require a good degree of fitness and skill, they are not fitness sports. Probably the most notable exceptions are soccer and basketball, provided they are played for at least forty-five minutes and at a fairly constant pace.

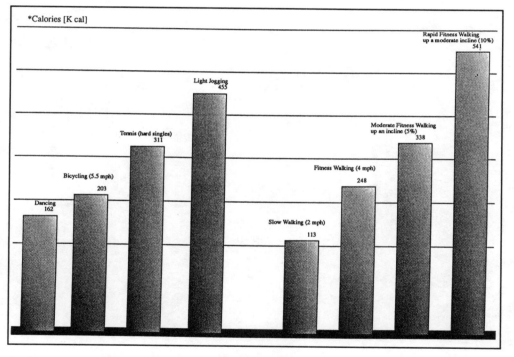

Calories [K cal]

Rapid Fitness Walking up a moderate incline (10%) 541

Light Jogging 455

Tennis (hard singles) 311

Bicycling (5.5 mph) 203

Dancing 162

Slow Walking (2 mph) 113

Fitness Walking (4 mph) 248

Moderate Fitness Walking up an incline (5%) 338

Calories expended during a typical forty-five-minute session for an average male (150 pounds). An average female (124 pounds) would burn 20% fewer calories.

CHAPTER 7

Walking Fundamentals

Walking is man's best medicine.
Hippocrates

Since most of us have been walking since we were about two years old, there is no need to explain the act of walking. Indeed, it is as automatic as breathing. I think that to complicate something as inherently simple and pure as walking is just short of sinful. But we do tend to grow into bad habits and are left oblivious to them until we are told better or discover them for ourselves. So, guilty of hypocrisy, I will suggest some "basics" to make your walk safer, more comfortable, and, naturally, more of a joy!

❗ STRETCHING

As mentioned previously, stretching is easiest and safest when the body is warm. A ten-minute hot shower or the same amount of *slow* walking will prepare you for stretching. Once you are sufficiently warm, find a plot of grass and complete your stretching routine. Done properly, stretching is your best way to avoid injuries. Moreover, it helps the body to wake up. Begin each day with stretching even when you do not walk, and you may find yourself no longer needing your daily shots of caffeine.

STRETCH IN MOTION

Once you've completed your pre-stretch, begin your walking. As you walk, you may feel tightness in specific areas. I frequently need to stretch my calves because of all the hills in San Francisco. So when you come to a light post, mailbox, or tree, stretch out whatever you need to and be on your way. Jog in place at stoplights, swing your arms, roll your head — above all, stay loose.

❗ CORRECT WALKING FORM

POSTURE

Doubtless, you have at some point in your life been admonished to "Stop slouching!" Well, the same goes for walking. Without an erect stance — the head and torso aligned over the lower body — it is quite difficult for oxygen and blood to circulate properly. It is important to keep the head high, the back straight, and the stomach and buttocks pulled in. Don't overdo it; you are not in the military. But if your eyes look far forward, your head will remain in the proper position and everything else should follow naturally.

ARM SWING

It is an old test indeed, but if you do not think that your arm swing is essential to proper walking, try trudging up a hill with your hands in your pockets. Within twenty yards or so, enlightenment will quickly come upon you. And if it doesn't, you're cheating! (See photos 53, 54.)

What has happened is that you have disrupted your body's internal rhythm. If you trust your instincts when walking, you will find that they know better. A full arm swing serves various functions. First, it acts like a pump, pulsing blood throughout your heart and lungs. Second, as your left leg goes back to push off, your right arm maintains the momentum you have established. A analogous situation can be experienced while swimming. When you down stroke, you do not lose forward momentum (if you are swimming properly) because your legs are constantly thrusting you forward. And finally, your upper body gets a workout and increases your metabolism when your arms are moving with your body.

53. *An exhausting walk uphill. Notice the long pendulum swings and the full breathing.*

54. *Notice the arms. This is almost like walking uphill with your hands in your pockets. He's losing forward momentum with each step because the hands are not doing a thing.*

FORWARD MOVEMENT

When you walk, be aware of the direction you are going. Do not let yourself become a listing ship unhelmed. Your arm swing is your rudder. To walk *efficiently*, swing your arms straight out in front of your body with your open palm pointing straight behind you. If you have run a lot or aerobicized in the past, you may find that your torso is going side to side and not straight ahead. A simple test to determine this is to wear a day pack on your back with a moderate amount of weight and concentrate on the movement of the pack on your back. If you feel the pack moving side to side as you walk, your upper body is doing the same thing. Adjust the swing of your arms so that the palms are open and facing directly behind you. Make small adjustments until the pack is virtually still on your back, and you will be on your way to a well-helmed and an efficient walk.

55. *A joy to stride with Exerstrider™ and friends. The length of your stride feels like it's being lengthened.*

STRIDE AND PACE — NOT THE SAME THING

Again, your body knows best. Your stride will adjust in accordance with your pace (number of steps per mile). To determine your natural stride, stand with your feet together and let yourself fall forward. As you step to catch your fall, you will determine your natural stride.

Your pace is determined by the number of steps you take per given unit of time. In walking, we measure our pace in miles per hour. A slow pace is three miles per hour, moderate is four miles per hour, and fast is five miles per hour. Walking any faster becomes inefficient. At this rate, physiology indicates that it is actually more efficient to run or race walk. Nevertheless, most walkers improve their cardiovascular systems by building and maintaining a consistent, brisk pace. The tendency of neophytes is to overdo it from the start and develop fatigue or injuries that abruptly ends their new walking campaign. Listen to your body. Are you gasping for breath? Can you carry on a conversation with a friend? Be patient; your endurance will improve if you stick with it. A caveat: Three days in a row without walking and you will feel the loss. Make walking a regular part of each day and you will reap consistent benefits.

❢ ALTER YOUR WALKING TERRAIN

Whenever you walk on one type of terrain for a long period of time, you may notice that you develop tightness in a particular area of your body.

For instance, when I walk up a long, low-grade stretch of road for a mile or so, I develop tightness in my shins. This is a minor inconvenience that can be solved by stretching the shin every one hundred yards or so. However, there is always a potential risk of developing chronically sore or strained muscles, and, if it is prolonged, you may develop tendinitis.

Muscles need a variety of movements for maximum benefit. You may notice when you are typing, washing a car, or doing anything requiring the same movement over and over again that you develop muscle fatigue. You also have a potential for carpal tunnel syndrome (a repetitive motion ailment of the joints).

Seek variety. It is far better to integrate into your walking hills, flatlands, and a set of stairs or two, than it is to walk mile after mile on a long flat road. Your walk also has the promise of being more visually stimulating. Indeed, your mind may develop mental fatigue due to the sameness of your terrain if you don't vary it.

WALKING DOWNHILL

A long time ago, before I nearly ripped the cartilage in my knee, I used to gallop (my term for walking fast and out of control) down hills. Well, I don't do that anymore.

There is a "home stretch" tendency that may occur after you have walked up steep terrain for a while. DO NOT GIVE IN TO IT. Walking downhill is more dangerous and more strenuous on the joints and lower back than any other walking terrain. The grade and gravity together place an enormous strain on you, treating you in effect like a human shock absorber.

In fact, on the steepest of hills, I recommend that you traverse them. Even if you have good, healthy knees today, they are among the most fragile, poorly designed parts of the body — so take care of them.

 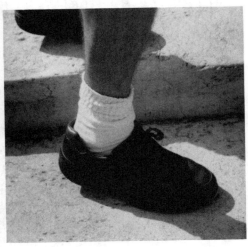

56. *A dangerous way to walk down stairs. A few inches farther and you may find yourself sliding down the rest of them.*

57. *A safe way to plant your foot on stairs. You have more control, and your knee is less likely to buckle if you do slip.*

STAIRS

When walking down stairs it is safest to put as much of the shoe's surface as possible on each stair. How often have you seen someone step off the edge of a stair and then slide down a few feet on his backside, usually using bare hands to stop? (Little pebbles from concrete stairs embedded in the hand are very painful!)

For this reason, place each step so that the foot is at about a 45° angle to each stair. However, keep your torso parallel to your direction of travel. Only your feet and legs pivot. (See photos 56, 57.)

❗ COOL DOWN

Allowing yourself to cool down after your walk is most important. Just as warming up prepares you for your walk, cooling down prepares you for your next one. It does this by keeping your muscles from tightening up as your heart returns to its resting level. Also, ask yourself how you feel. You may need a day off or a lighter walk the next day. Be a smart walker and you will stay strides ahead in your walks for fitness, mental health, and fulfillment.

❗ WALKING OBSTACLES

When learning to drive we are taught about the importance of "high aim steering," or focusing far in the distance to see where trouble may await. When walking, we need to aim high *and* low, left *and* right, especially in metropolitan areas. Obstacles are all around, so awareness is the key to safety.

Ditches/construction signs. Just as cars slow down when there is construction being done, so must you. Look above you to see what is happening. Remember, you do not have a steel shell around you. It is easy to feel free and uninhibited by what is going on around you, and it is a relief not to be stuck in traffic and to be able to keep moving. However, keep these feelings at bay and be alert.

Branches and holes. When walking through uncharted, non-trailed wilderness, be absolutely sure of what you step on with each foot. A small rock, a branch, or a hole could put you out of commission from walking and perhaps a whole lot more. (See photo 58.)

Surfaces. Always be aware of where you are stepping. Not only will you avoid "smelly shoes," but you will keep those precious ankles from going out of commission, which could happen if you step on something that sends you to the ground. In city walking, the uprooted sidewalk is one of the most common threats to pedestrians. Be aware of them. When in the back woods, try to stay on the marked trails at all times. Should your temptation to go exploring become irresistible, then watch each step. Roots, holes, rocks, water, bottles, etc., may upend you and cause injury. (See photo 59.)

Walk against traffic. Walking against traffic is an old rule of thumb. Not only can motorists see you better, but you are able to take evasive action to avoid a car, should it be necessary. Also, when walking on the side of a road with vehicle traffic, you should wear bright colors — white, yellow, or red. (See photo 60.)

58. When walking in the wilderness, always look where you are stepping. Forest litter can twist an ankle in no time if you aren't paying attention.

59. The infamous sidewalk lip. Everyone has tripped on it; walkers beware. If you see a tree along the sidewalk, be especially careful. It's a good indication that a root may have buckled the sidewalk where you are walking.

60. Always walk against traffic when you're on the road. Also, increase your visibility by wearing bright colors and a reflector vest. Be a safe walker.

Walking at night. Walking at night is not a good idea. According to police accounts, in more than 85% of the cases in which motorists killed pedestrians, the motorist claimed not to have seen the pedestrian in time to stop. Walking at night is especially not recommended for a woman or a child alone. If, however, there is no other time in the day, do walk with a group of people and do wear a reflective vest. If you have a dog, walk with him. His strong sense of smell will serve you well should there be thugs encroaching. It is also a good idea to carry a flashlight and to stay out of poorly lit areas.

Dogs. Avoid a clash with a threatening canine. The safest encounter is no encounter at all, especially if the dog's owner is not in sight. If you do wind up striding into a dog's territory, take it slow. *Do not run.* A firm "GO HOME!" may work. Or you can carry one of various dog repellents or a noisemaker if neighborhood dogs become a daily nuisance.

Headphones. A Walkman™ can add enjoyment and fluid rhythm to your walking. But it also makes your ears oblivious to the outside world at a time when you may need them most. As a general rule, never use your stereo when walking through the city. Horns, sirens, and voices are your signals to look out. If you cannot hear them, you could cause a serious accident involving more people than yourself.

Birds. There have been several occasions when I have been approaching a feeding flock of pigeons, a little boy screamed as loud as he could, and a squadron of birds instantly launched into flight, heading my way.

Never assume that they are going to fly over you. Stop, cross your arms, and put them over your face. The birds may appear small, but a pigeon missile in the face can ruin an afternoon!

CHAPTER 8

A Healthy Diet

I love bookstores. When I'm not working, walking, or writing, I usually have my nose buried in a stack of books somewhere. Over the years I have made some observations about the layout of bookstores. I am convinced that the diet section of bookstores should be moved to the humor section. No joke. I laugh at the absurdity, the fads, and the myths that countless weight and diet gurus feed the public. Following is my chronicle of the funniest jokes I have found in the diet section of bookstores.

1. *Put your fork down after every three bites, wait for a minute, and then take another bite.* I figure it would take about seventy minutes to eat a New York strip steak!

2. *Never clear your plate.* And live with your conscience for throwing away perfectly good food several times a day.

3. *Hold food in your mouth for two minutes so you no longer like the taste of it.* Then starve to death when you have successfully conditioned yourself to hate food!

4. *Use a small plate and fork to make small portions look larger* . . . and a large table to catch the dribbles!

All joking aside, your health and weight are no laughing matter. Quick-fix weight loss programs are dangerous because they tend to be solely concerned with weight loss and not concerned with overall fitness.

Fitness must combine a sensible diet with a regular exercise program. Good eating habits, typically established early in life, are the best way to increase your longevity. How many overweight ninety year olds do you see waddling down the street?

❗ OVERWEIGHT?

Here's a question for you. What is something that few people want, but millions seem to have?

Give up?

Too much body fat.

Americans consume more fat and sugar than any other country in the world. As a result, there are sixty to seventy million adults and ten to twelve million school-age children in the United States who are too fat.

WHAT CAUSES THIS OVERWEIGHT CONDITION?

The most common cause of obesity is simple. When more calories are consumed than are burned, the excess is stored as fat. Because of America's ability to produce an abundance of food, coupled with modern technology that has developed labor-saving machines, the physical effort required in daily work life has decreased. This has, in part, led to a near epidemic of weight problems in our country.

Up until recently, opinion held that obesity was caused by overeating. However, new evidence proves that a lack of regular physical activity is the real culprit. The overweight do not necessarily eat more than their normal-weight counterparts, they are just less active.

With age and decreased activity, muscle tissue gradually deteriorates. Less muscle, combined with the gradual accumulation of stored body fat, initiates a rapid change in one's body fat percentage. If you maintain unhealthful eating habits as you get older and decrease your level of physical activity, you are almost certain to accumulate excess body fat.

THE PSYCHOLOGICAL EFFECT

Being overweight is a danger to your health; still, the American stigma attributed to being overweight is troubling.

If you are overweight, you are generally perceived to be unattractive, not sexy, inadequate, undisciplined, lazy, insecure, and even depressed. Indeed, heavyset people tend to have weak personalities, higher anxiety levels, and lower self-esteem than people of normal weight. Consequently, the overweight encounter excessive teasing, ridicule, prejudice, and rejection. Moreover, as they are prone to low self-esteem, they may encounter psychological problems such as poor body image, a sense of failure, a passive/defeatist approach to life situations, and an uncommon anticipation of rejection.

❗ BODY FAT

In the United States there are many physical, social, and psychological problems associated with too much body fat. Many Americans are obsessed with being thin. In some cultures, though, obesity is a social advantage — indeed, a sign of prosperity and health. Have you browsed through *Vanity Fair* lately? When you see the thin models in the ads, you will know that this is not the case in America.

There are many health reasons for avoiding obesity. It is associated with several heart disease risk factors, including high blood pressure, high cholesterol, and diabetes. In addition, strokes and kidney problems are frequently linked to obesity, as are certain cancers such as breast cancer in women, and prostate and colon cancer in men.

DECREASED LIFE SPAN

Moreover, obesity has contributed to a shorter life span in life expectancy studies. Research indicates that moderately overweight people may increase the risk of having a life span short of life expectancy (seventy-five years) by as much as 40%. Obesity may result in a life span reduced by nearly 70%.

WHAT CAN BE DONE ABOUT EXCESS BODY FAT?

For your weight to remain constant, you must use up as many calories as you take in. When the amounts are not balanced, your weight changes. There are approximately 3,500 calories in one pound of stored body fat. Let us suppose that you take in an extra 500 calories a day; you will gain about one

FOOTSTEPS

What's Your Cholesterol Level?

The National Institute of Health and The American Heart Association recommend that you have regular cholesterol checks. Following are the National Institute of Health's guidelines for blood cholesterol levels, in mg/dL.

Risk	20-29 Years Old	30-39 Years Old	40+ Years Old
Average	Below 200	Below 220	Below 240
Moderate	200-220	220-240	240-260
High	Above 220	Above 240	Above 260

pound of body fat every seven days. Of course, the reverse is true. If you take in 500 calories less a day than you need, you will lose about one pound every seven days.

The healthiest and most effective way to lose body fat is to maintain a well-balanced diet combined with regular, moderate exercise.

A well-balanced diet is your source of energy. It should consist of foods high in essential nutrients and prepared free of excess fats. If these nutrients are missing, your body will not function properly.

Exercise burns calories. When you use your muscles, they require energy, so the more your muscles contract, the more calories you consume. Doctors concur that exercise is the key to increasing lean body weight — turning fat to muscle. The failure rate of many dieting plans is high because exercise is not included in their weight management programs.

A WORD ON SPOT REDUCTION

It is a common misconception that you can lose weight from a specific area of your body by working that specific body part. Many people err in thinking that by doing countless sit-ups, they will remove fat from the abdominal area. Regrettably, spot reduction does not work. Localized exercises, however, will help to build muscle underneath the body fat, and in doing so will actually shrink the tissue underneath the fat, since muscle tissue is more condensed than fat tissue.

❗ GOOD FOOD MAKES GOOD SENSE

Have you ever decided to spoil your car and fill it up with 92% octane fuel? Costs a bit more, but it's worth it, right? To get the most from your body, you need to fill it with premium fuel.

Certainly you have heard it before. You are what you eat. Most every food stimulates chemical production in your brain. Norepinephrine, a "feel good" enzyme, enhances our sense of well-being, our alertness, and our ability to solve problems. Combined with a vigorous walk, which also stimulates enzyme production, eating good foods provides us with a high that make us feel good.

Whenever I, having had a sensible morning breakfast, take to the dew-covered streets, my mind stimulates my body and wakes me better than a cup of coffee does.

COMPLEX CARBOHYDRATES

Fruits, vegetables, and whole grains will take your body a long way. The less food is processed, the better.

Wholesome foods, straight from Mother Nature (raw vegetables, fruits, and grains) with peelings and all, are going to give your body the most nutrition of any food. It is difficult to eat too many raw carbohydrates. Only carbohydrates burn 100% clean and efficiently.

FIBER

A diet with adequate fiber keeps the human engine clean, while impeding the absorption of cholesterol into our bodies. The American diet is notorious for having an insufficient supply of fiber. Again, modern pulverization of our food removes the most essential elements of our food fuel. Fancy cakes and breads do not provide your body the type of fiber it needs. Wheat bran, whole wheat, oats, and high-fiber cereals will.

FAT

There are two types of fat — animal and vegetable, or saturated and unsaturated. Cholesterol levels are increased by animal (saturated) fats like butter, red meat, and cheese. Vegetable fat is unsaturated and actually lowers cholesterol levels in the blood. A good rule to remember is that foods high in fat are high in cholesterol as well.

Animal fats ultimately slow you down. Included in this group are meats, fried food, oil-based condiments, candy and chocolates, and bacon and other fatty pork. Avoid these and instead substitute fruit, vegetable dishes, and whole grain breads and cereals. To confuse the issue, though, two of the worst saturated fats are from coconut oil and palm oil, *not* animal fats.

Recent studies suggest that walking may decrease the animal fat producing cholesterol (LDL), while simultaneously increasing the amount of vegetable cholesterol (HDL), which helps break up plaque that settles on artery walls.

JUNK THE JUNK

America has an enormous appetite for processed, unnatural, and unwholesome junk food. Candy, soft drinks, chips, and artificial food concoctions have become staple between-meal snacks. These sugar- and chemical-loaded snacks give you a short-term energy boost, but ultimately slow you down and add bulges to your waistline.

Instead, try foods that are good for you, such as potatoes, raw vegetables, fruits, low-fat dairy products (skim milk), and whole-grain breads.

❗ WALK AFTER MEALS

Spaghetti, garlic bread, double-baked potato, more bread, more spaghetti, salad, coffee, more bread, dessert. Admittedly an extremely heavy meal, but many people will eat just like that. Can you imagine feeling a little tired after finishing? Well, you will once you sit or lie down. When you finish eating, your body begins to sap your energy to break down the feast you have consumed. This drain typically makes you feel sluggish and unmotivated to do anything requiring energy. However, instead of watching television or sitting around, go on a walk. It helps you to digest your food, gives you renewed energy, relieves the bloated feeling you may have, tends to suppress your desire for more food, and is a great way to avoid the temptation of a fattening dessert and an after-dinner brandy.

❢ GRAZE AWAY

Eat five or six smaller meals each day *instead* of a typical huge American meal. Grazing, however, should not be confused with snacking. Eat smaller meals several times a day. Eat wholesome foods, but make sure you always have a supply of fruits and vegetables nearby to reduce the temptation to buy a Hershey bar at a vending machine.

I am amazed when I go to a coffee shop early in the morning and see a businessman beginning his day with fried eggs, buttered toast, ham, and coffee. Not only is this meal loaded with cholesterol and fat, but it quickly decreases your energy.

If this rings familiar, try being creative with some oatmeal (yes, oatmeal!), fresh fruit or fruit juice, and a bran muffin. After a day or so you will find that your energy level is no longer sapped at mid-morning.

GRAZE AS YOU WALK

As you walk, you burn large amounts of energy. On longer walks, carry some grazing food. Bananas, apples, cold baked potatoes, rice cakes, trail mix, and carrots are loaded with nutrients and energy and are easily transportable.

❢ POISONOUS HABITS

Don't smoke! According to former Surgeon General C. Everett Koop, smoking cigarettes is the single greatest cause of preventable deaths in the United States. Smoking a pack a day, never mind living in an asphyxiating metropolis, may very well triple the likelihood of a heart attack and cause irreparable damage to lung tissue.

My strong convictions against the rhythmic savagery of inhaling nicotine and smoke have had a singular effect on those closest to me. Getting my friends to quit smoking has

61. *Grazing on the road. Bananas, trail mix, and carrots are nutritious and easy to carry.*

always been among my most profound convictions and has demonstrated, to my delight, the immediate way in which an opinion, if expressed strongly enough, can have practical results.

What is peculiar and ironic to many non-smokers, indeed, is to see people, especially our friends, smoke, yet eat well and dedicate themselves to 5 A.M. wake-up calls to go to the fitness club. What I notice, however, is that very few smokers participate in any aerobic activity. Their soot-coated lungs are not capable of generating enough oxygen to fuel their bodies.

Thus afflicted, they regularly experience shortness of breath and/or chronic coughing. A smoker's oxygen-transport-ability is tremendously reduced due to the smoke's carbon dioxide replacing the blood's oxygen. It is somewhat analogous to filling a gas tank full of water to the point where there is no more room for fuel.

The good news is that it is never too late to stop. Indeed, the benefits of quitting, even after decades of smoking, are dramatic. It is estimated that the likelihood of heart failure is cut in half after being smoke-free for one year. And while ambling purposefully cannot stop people from smoking, the discipline that impels people to walk can be harnessed to stop this destructive, and often deadly, habit.

REPLACE A DRINK WITH A WALK

If you are a mild to moderate drinker who enjoys a drink each day after work, you may notice your waistline getting larger and your stamina being sapped. Many of the "desirable" effects of consuming alcohol can be achieved by a half-hour of walking. While the alcohol "high" will ultimately make you lethargic, the walker's high stimulates the production of chemical neural enzymes that revitalize you and leave you feeling calm and at ease.

CHAPTER 9

Experiencing Pain or Discomfort

The expression "No pain, no gain" is a myth. It is not necessary to feel pain or discomfort to become fit and healthy. On the contrary, mild exercise is the best exercise. We are often so impatient that we look for immediate results in our fitness programs — we think that the harder and faster and more painful our workout is, the greater the benefit we will derive. Nonsense! Over-training only discourages and frustrates! It causes sore and strained muscles, tired feet, and worn-out feelings.

Pain should not be a part of your walking workout. If you do experience pain, your body is sending a signal to you that you should not ignore. Try to narrow down what your problem is and consult your doctor for a proper diagnosis.

On the other hand, there may be some discomforts associated with walking that cannot be avoided. But you should be able to lessen them, if not get rid of them altogether. This chapter will distinguish between the two.

❗ SERIOUS PROBLEMS

ACHING BACK

Back pain is almost a universal problem. An estimated 80% of the population suffers from back pain at some point in their life. Bed rest was once considered the prescribed method for dealing with it. Now, however, the medical consensus suggests that if your back hurts, it may be time for a walk.

Anything that alters your center of gravity — poor posture, pot belly, pregnancy, walking with a heavy backpack — increases the stress on the joints of the back. For those with mild back pain, being inactive is often the worst thing you can do (rather, not do) to alleviate discomfort. Combined with good posture — head held high, the back straight, and the stomach and the buttocks pulled in — walking strengthens the abdominal muscles, which help support the back.

Indeed, I called upon a podiatrist, who diagnosed that my spine was slightly curved, thus the cause of my aching back. A pair of custom orthotics was prescribed, and I have been walking pain-free ever since. At any rate, regular stretching, combined with long, easy walks, may be the best medicine you can give your back.

People with more acute pain, however, should consult a doctor before engaging in any physical activity/therapy.

CHEST PAIN

Not a pain to be taken lightly, your chest could be plagued by something as benign as indigestion or as dangerous as angina pectoris or an insufficient supply of blood to the heart muscle. If your pain persists, see your doctor. It may be nothing at all, but do not wait to find out.

KNEE PAIN

Orthopedists have long considered the knee to be the poorest designed joint in the body. Just about any physical activity you do on it is stressful. Watch a football game and see how many knees go out in a single game!

Overuse, a muscular imbalance, foot dysfunction, or poor walking form can cause the knee to ache. If you are overweight, pregnant, or out of shape, you are likely to have a case of the sore knee the next morning. Sometimes, it may be wise to invest in a stable, well-cushioned shoe. Almost always, however, decreased mileage is the best cure. Once again, do not overdo it too early on. Dormant muscles and joints need time to wake up.

HEAT STROKE

Heat stroke can catch up to you before you realize it. Symptoms include lightheadedness, hot-feeling skin, weakness, nausea, faintness, and extreme thirst. To avoid heat stroke, drink lots of water and give your body time to get used to the heat by gradually increasing the length of your walk. It may take as much as two weeks for an adjustment. When the temperature is high, you feel hotter than an actual thermometer reading due to the relative humidity.

HYPOTHERMIA

This occurs when you lose warmth from the core of your body. Lighter weight people and women are more apt to suffer from hypothermia. One of the most dangerous aspects of hypothermia is that its victims seldom realize they are being struck. Symptoms include loss of coordination, violent shivering, blue lips, slurred speech, and incoherence.

For treatment, get the victim to a warm and dry area away from the elements. If there are two other walkers, they can "sandwich" the victim between themselves. Warm food and fluids should be administered to reestablish body warmth. Once recovered, the victim should avoid exertion and be monitored for a possible relapse.

❢ WALKING HAZARDS

SPRAINS

Sprains account for three-quarters of joggers' ankle injuries. This may cause a number of problems, including arch and heel pain, as well as heel spurs. A temporary insert or custom-made orthotic may remedy the over-pronation.

I well remember the first sprain I had when I began endurance walking several years ago. The problem, as I was to discover, was that my shoes did not fit — they were too loose. Loose shoes allow the foot to slip and slide within the shoe. As I was walking hard around a corner, my foot twisted right out of the shoe and landed sideways on the pavement. The point of the story: Wear shoes that fit!

Most of the time sprains are a result of not looking where you are going. Curbs, uneven pavement, tree roots, and other natural obstacles are your ankles' worst enemies, so look out for them.

Swelling is the best way to determine the severity of the sprain. If you think it may be a severe sprain, if you hear a pop or cannot walk, remember the word RICE, used in the sports profession — Rest the ankle, put Ice on it, use Compression such as an Ace™ bandage, and Elevate it to decrease the blood flow to the area.

Gradual walking, as soon as the ankle will bear weight again, is the best way to strengthen the ankle. Throughout rehabilitation, be aware of your limitations. Going one step beyond your present capabilities can reaggravate your injury and send you right back where you started.

DOG BITES

If a dog bite breaks the skin, apply direct pressure to the wound to stop the bleeding and get to a medical facility promptly. You may need a rabies shot. Try to contact the dog's owner to determine if the dog has had shots recently. The more information you can give the treating physician, the better.

INSECT BITES

Ticks are usually founds in brush and bushes. Once they have clung to you, it usually takes six hours for them to latch into the skin for feeding. If you periodically check your body and especially your hairline (this is their favorite feeding area), you should get them before they latch on and transmit any diseases. Unfortunately, they are very subtle diggers, so it is difficult to feel them bite. If you do find a tick on your body, grasp it well with a pair of tweezers close to the skin and pull it out firmly. Disinfect the area of attachment and watch for possible redness, swelling, headache, and nausea.

Ticks can transmit Rocky Mountain spotted fever, Lyme disease, and tularemia — all of which are quite serious and require a call to your doctor for treatment. The HIV virus is believed not to be transmitted by ticks because once they select a victim, they will not remove their head from that body. They die upon extraction.

Also, whenever you set a piece of clothing on a trail covered with forest litter (pine needles, leaves, etc.), be sure to shake it out thoroughly. I once found a tick in my hair after having worn my cap all day; it provided a dark and safe environment for the blood-sucking insect.

Like gnats and black flies, most mosquitoes are out for your blood. They love warm, moist air, so stay away from swamps and marshes. The best thing you can do to avoid them is to use repellents and wear long clothing.

An aerosol, clothing-only spray called Permanone has been tested by the U.S. Army on its apparel with good results. Due to regulations, it is not available in all states, but you can call the manufacturer, Coulston International (215/253-0167) to determine its current availability.

❢ POSSIBLE DISCOMFORTS

SHIN SORENESS

Shin soreness, also known as shin splints, may be caused by an outward toeing of the feet or an inflamed tendon in the lower leg. Walking faster with an elongated step or walking up steep hills often causes shin soreness because these muscles rarely get much use. Well-padded, properly fitted walking shoes can be the answer. Also, toeing the tip of the foot back and forth into the ground may help stretch that area very well.

SIDE STITCH

If you have ever run long and fast or competitively, you are familiar with a side stitch. It is a severe cramp often located in the upper abdomen on the left side.

If a stitch occurs, slow your pace, breathe deeply, and place your hands on top of your head. Also, try bending forward and taking hard, pursing breaths. Direct pressure with the fingers on the area with the side stitch may also relieve the pain.

To avoid stitches altogether, avoid foods that produce gas, do as many sit-ups as you can, and as you get into better shape, side stitches should be a pain of the past.

CRAMPS

Muscle cramps are strong, temporary contractions of muscles. When I ran in high school, nothing I experienced was more painful than coping with a cramp for a mile or more.

The best preventive medicine is to be well-hydrated, warm up before exercising, and strengthen all of your muscle groups. To treat cramps, stop and gently stretch the muscle that is cramped. If you are getting a lot of cramps despite your best efforts, consult with your doctor. You may have a chemical imbalance.

ALLERGIES/HAY FEVER

For most of its victims, allergies and hay fever are a nuisance. The best way to avoid them is to avoid what ails you — assuming you know what does. If you do not, and you begin to wheeze, take note of the landscape. What type of plants are there? Is there a lot of dust in the air? Does the allergy occur during the summer or fall, when most weeds bloom? An allergy shot just prior to the allergy season may be your best hope of having comfortable walks. Over-the-counter medication, prescription antihistamines, or steroid nasal sprays should also be considered.

❗ FOOT CARE

Despite the fact that walking is one of the least stressful exercises, I can attest to the fact that some foot irritation, even severe pain, may develop as you begin a regular walking program. With twenty-six tiny bones, little muscles, tendons, and ligaments, there are many areas where minor irritation or pain can crop up.

Indeed, about fifty-five million of us have trouble with our feet — from corns, blisters, calluses, bunions, and ingrown toenails, to athlete's foot, cramps, painful arches, and the list goes on.

Fortunately, nearly every foot problem is 100% treatable through either home remedies or a professional cure from a podiatrist.

As for myself, I began to feel excruciating pain in my toes and arches when I began walking longer distances (fifteen miles or more). At first I thought the discomfort was due to the shoes I was wearing. I bought a new pair of walking shoes, broke them in, and the pain was still there. I made an appointment to see the podiatrist.

A VISIT TO THE PODIATRIST

The doctor first probed my feet for about twenty minutes. Pushing, pulling, tapping, prodding, and asking, "Does this hurt?", "How does this feel?", and various other tedious questions.

Having determined where my pain was located, the doctor ordered about six X-rays to get a deeper look into my feet. What did she find? Arthritis! I could not believe it. Due to a slight curvature in my spine, which I have had since birth, she determined that my feet were bearing slightly uneven weights. Over a period of twenty years, this had caused unusual stress on my toes and arches. I was prescribed a pair of orthotics to correct my dysfunctional feet.

To make the orthotics, a plaster mold is taken of the foot. It feels like a cast is being applied to your foot, but it is removed before it dries permanently.

On my next visit, the plaster mold had been used to create my new, custom-fitted orthotics. When I tried them on, I was convinced that they were made for another patient. I felt protrusions and gaps in all the wrong places. I was told it would take time to adapt to them. In hindsight, I can best describe a pair of new orthotics as like having braces put on your teeth. They feel all wrong, but they are there to correct a problem.

After about a month of gradually increased use, my orthotics felt like a natural extension of my feet. My pain had completely disappeared and, following some extensive ultrasound treatment, I was back on the road trekking my usual eight miles at dawn.

❗ FOOT PROBLEMS

ACHILLES TENDINITIS

The Achilles tendon is the ligament cord at the back of the ankle that connects the calf muscles to the heel bone. If it is inflexible or over-stressed, it may become inflamed and irritated. A heel lift or other correction in your shoe may relieve this pressure.

ATHLETE'S FOOT

Also called ringworm, athlete's foot is a surface fungal infection on the skin of the feet. Untreated, dangerous secondary infections may occur.

1. Wash thoroughly in between the toes each day with mild soap. Be sure to dry the toes and feet thoroughly.
2. If you are susceptible to an infection, apply an anti-fungal powder daily in between the toes and in the socks.
3. Always wear cotton socks. Synthetic socks tend to create heat — an environment where the athlete's foot fungi thrive.
4. Wear shoes that breathe well. Change your shoes and socks daily.
5. After a day's use, air out your shoes for at least twenty-four hours and apply an antiseptic spray such as Desenex™ before wearing again.

BLISTERS

We all dread this accumulation of water under the skin. Blisters are created by two elements — heat and friction. The skin reacts by cooling the area with a pocket of water that ultimately creates more pain for us. The best way to cope with blisters is never to get them.

If, despite your efforts, you still get a blister, treat it properly and you will minimize further pain and a possible infection.

Use an ice pack, whether at home or on the road, to numb the area of the blister. This will help alleviate the pain. To drain the blister, sterilize a sewing needle (or use a syringe) with rubbing alcohol and then swab the blister with alcohol also. Puncture it in several places and gently squeeze the fluid out from all sides until it appears to be fairly well drained. Leave the skin of the blister intact. Do not try to remove it since this will expose raw and as yet unprotected skin underneath the blister roof.

For a blister on the bottom of the foot, cut a round piece of moleskin with an inner circle removed to expose the blister. Place the moleskin over the blister so the blister is exposed. For a toe blister, the same procedure should be followed, with the addition of an application of sterile gauze. This prevents the toe blister from nudging the toe box of your shoe. A blister should receive a light application of iodine to prevent infection.

CALLUSES

Calluses are an accumulation of thick, dead skin. This is your body's attempt to protect the skin from irritation. Calluses serve a practical function; do not treat them unless they give you problems.

If they do, try using medicated pads, pumice stones, or lotions with urea, or soaking the foot in warm water.

As the calluses begin to wear and skin spurs develop, use a pair of cuticle scissors or a toenail cutter to remove them.

FOREIGN BODIES

What is a foreign body? Anything that gets stuck in your foot and does not belong there. The most common objects are splinters and glass.

If you cannot remove the object yourself, or if it begins to swell and redden, see a podiatrist or a physician as soon as possible.

Although various home treatment procedures exist, I will not endorse one. Removing a foreign object from underneath your skin is a form of surgery. I urge you to consult a physician or podiatrist before attempting to remove any deeply embedded foreign object from the skin by yourself.

HEEL PAIN

Heel pain can be caused in various ways. A bone bruise is quite common and is caused by a sharp impact of a hard object against the foot. This inflammation of the heel bone makes it extremely painful to walk or run.

Nerve inflammation is caused by consistent, hard pressure on parts of the foot. It may be remedied by foot therapy, including ultrasound and foot shock treatment. Once the foot has healed, special heel inserts of orthotics may be used to absorb the shock against the heel in the future.

HEEL SPUR

A heel spur is a shelf of bone, usually the entire width of the heel bone, formed by the continuous tearing away of the lining of the heel bone.

If icing the foot does not provide any relief (see the icing procedure in the foot therapy section), an orthotic to keep the heel in place may be necessary. Other treatments include physical therapy and/or medications.

INGROWN TOENAILS

If you do not already own a pair, buy some toenail clippers. Ingrown toenails are usually caused by neglect. If a remedy is needed, gently lift the edge of the nail with a cuticle stick or your fingernail and place a piece of cotton between the nail and the skin. Avoid liquid remedies that shrink the skin. In a few days you should be able to trim the nail with scissors or clippers. Inspect toenails daily and keep them trimmed.

OVERPRONATION

A normal foot rolls inward and down when it strikes the ground to absorb shock and to maintain balance. Overpronation occurs when the leg and foot turn inward too far. If you overpronate, the force created when your foot hits the ground is not in alignment with the leg. This places stress on the whole body and may cause injury.

As a sign of this, you may find excessive wear on the inner sides of your shoes. In high school you may have been razzed as "pigeon toed." However, this aberration, too, can be corrected with custom orthotics.

SESMOIDITIS

This is a clinical term for pain in the ball of the foot. Something that I have experienced, this is a condition in which two tiny bones in the foot below the first metatarsals become bruised. Sometimes drugstore pads will do the job, but alas, not in my case. If they are not enough, you should consult a podiatrist.

❗ *FOOT THERAPY*

MASSAGE

Early in your new walking routine, you are likely to experience foot, calf, and shin soreness. Soreness in the muscle is caused by a build-up of lactic acid in the muscles. Therapeutic massage improves the muscles' blood circulation and pumps the acid, thus reducing residual soreness.

You will find that foot massage is especially beneficial in relieving soreness of the feet. After a walk of several miles, the continuous pressure on the feet pushes down on blood vessels and reduces the flow of blood. Therapeutic foot massage opens the blood vessels and increases circulation.

FOOT BATH

For foot soreness and fatigue, contrast baths are extremely effective. You will need two containers in which the affected part of the foot can fit comfortably. The greater the temperature difference between the two containers, the greater the benefit. This will take some getting used to. Try gradually increasing or decreasing the temperature by adding hot water or ice, respectively, to each foot bath.

The cold bath will decrease pain and swelling. Obviously, you can expect the sensation of ice-cold water to be uncomfortable, but if your feet could talk (and I suppose they do in their own way) they would thank you for it.

Alter your foot baths as follows:

5 Minutes	=	Warm-Hot bath
1 Minute	=	Ice-Cold bath
4 Minutes	=	Warm-Hot bath
2 Minutes	=	Ice-Cold bath
3 Minutes	=	Warm-Hot bath
5 Minutes	=	Ice-Cold bath

At the end of this treatment, your foot may feel numb or tingly. This is quite normal. Just give your feet some time to regain normal temperature. Another simple, therapeutic exercise is to roll the bottom of your foot over a rolling pin for about five minutes on each foot. Until initial soreness and/or swelling go down, repeat at least once a day. In addition, powder your feet with talc or cornstarch. This is one of the best things you can do to revive your feet.

! LISTEN TO YOUR FEET

Listen to your feet just as you listen to the rest of your body. If you are feeling pain, try treating the problem at home. If you get no relief, see a podiatrist for a full examination.

I have developed a strong opinion, in light of my own experience, that at least a few foot examinations with a podiatrist should be made during the growth years and in the middle teens to determine if orthotics are necessary. A malformed or dysfunctional foot that is corrected early in life will save you years of pain, surgery, and money when your aching feet cannot take another bearable step.

Considering the weight your feet bear over a lifetime, give them the care and attention they have earned and deserve. They work hard for you.

CHAPTER 10

Special Case Walkers

❗ *THE ELDERLY*

Those who do not get around as quickly as they used to will want to consult with their physician before they embark on any exercise routine. A walking cane is a great companion for every walker, but it should be carried by all older walkers for more stability as well as for protection and fending off over-zealous canines.

OSTEOPOROSIS AND ARTHRITIS

Osteoporosis is a serious bone-thinning disease that causes pain, broken bones, stooped posture, and loss of weight, especially in the elderly. The best way to avoid or at least minimize its development is to introduce a calcium-rich diet or take calcium supplements to strengthen the bones and increase their mass. Avoid inactivity (get off the couch, stop watching television, etc.) and walk twice a day with as much stretching as possible in between walks.

Although the body's moans and groans may plead "No more!", walking is one of the best things you can do for your ailing bones. Try to walk, whether alone, with the help of Exerstriders, or with another person, for at least twenty minutes each day.

125

62. *Walking is an exercise you can do for the rest of your life.*

❗ *THE HEAVYSET*

Heavier-than-average people sometimes have a problem with chafing of the thighs and groin during walks. A simple solution to this problem is to lubricate the area before and after with lanolin or Vaseline™ to prevent inflammation of the skin. Also, wear larger-than-usual shorts or sweat pants to keep the area cool and dry. Carry a small supply of your lubricant on your walk to re-apply if necessary. You should always be able to find an inconspicuous place to apply it.

EXTREME OBESITY

Obesity abounds in our largely sedentary society. Typically, the obese have a larger inherent appetite than most people. The appestat, located in the hypothalamus of the brain, is believed to control the appetite. Unfortunately, the extremely obese have a very difficult time exercising for both physical and psychological reasons.

Two things must occur simultaneously. The diet must be curbed, and exercise — walking — must be done regularly. Even very slow walking is effective in bringing down the weight. Once again, if you experience chafing, use a lubricant and wear loose clothing to stay dry and cool. More important than speed or distance is endurance. Having achieved aerobic benefit from long, slow walking, your improvement will be obvious. From here, just keep at it and walk that weight off.

❗ SPECIAL HEALTH PROBLEMS

ARTHRITIS AND HIP PROBLEMS

Arthritis is a painful disease. Unfortunately, when people with arthritis or hip pain attempt to move about, the pain becomes a real obstacle and a disincentive to move. This is an unfortunate irony, for exactly what the joints need is movement to avoid becoming completely disabled due to atrophy and non-use. Some people have such severe cases that they must use swimming to lighten the load on their feet.

The first step, of course, is to get approval from your physician. Very slow walking is extremely beneficial to the arthritis sufferer. Do not let your pain fool you. With the help of your physician or a physical therapist, you can get up on your feet again and overcome the pain you feel.

HIGH BLOOD PRESSURE, HEART DISEASE, CANCER

Almost any bad health condition can be helped by the simple act of walking. It pulses your blood, breaks through the plaque in the arteries, rejuvenates tired and weak bones, and will help alleviate some psychosomatic disorders. Again, though, check with a doctor before beginning walking if you have any serious illness.

❗ PREGNANT WOMEN

Walking is an ideal activity for the pregnant woman. Many doctors recommend walking over most exercises because it does not put significant internal or external stress on the body. Obstetricians tend to concur that walking helps to keep pregnant women within their prescribed weight range since many of them tend to overeat.

Walking also prevents the swelling of the legs and ankles by maintaining proper blood circulation within the extremities. In addition, a sedentary soon-to-be mother is not going to bear the physical exertion of labor nearly as well as a healthy, walking woman.

When you do walk, it will help your lower back if you turn your hips up and out a bit to help support the extra weight. Avoid temperature extremes of any kind as this will put your body under stress that may affect the fetus. Walk slowly, but regularly, up to three times a week. Best of luck to you!

CHAPTER 11

Walking Profiles

If you are ready to leave father and mother, and brother and sister, and wife and children and friends, and never see them again, if you have paid your debts, and made your will, and settled all your affairs, and are a free man, then you are ready for a walk.
Henry David Thoreau

Most people are either unaware of or indifferent to those who have helped create, alter, and improve walking aids, walking products, and a greater understanding of walking itself. However, I ask that you consider for a moment the comfort (or discomfort) of the shoes you are wearing, the lines of athletic clothing and accessories that are available, and the break-throughs, or increased understanding of how the human body performs under varied conditions. Although you may not be interested in walking (which is not likely if you have gotten this far), the efforts of the following individuals and organizations have made their significant, indelible marks on the greater world of walking, the derivative knowledge, under-standing, and appreciation of the human body and mind, and the unique and mysterious linkage of the two.

! *BOB CARLSON*

The founder of Denver's Front Range Walkers and a former architect, Bob Carlson gave up his profession in the mid-1970s to devote his life to the promotion of health and physical fitness. Although he began by running marathons, he moved to walking and race walking in 1982. He has won many championships, such as the National Masters, normally completing the 5K in twenty-nine or thirty minutes. He has written extensively and taught the benefits of walking as the best all-around exercise.

! EDWARD PAYSON WESTON

Considered the most famous race walker in modern history, Edward Payson Weston inspired the country to get to its feet. He was known for crawling for miles through a blizzard, using a set of railroad tracks to guide himself during a 3,500 mile trek. At age eighty-five, Payson was still walking marathons and did so until his death in 1929. He was ninety.

! NATHAN PRITIKIN

Nathan Pritikin founded and directed the Longevity Center and the Pritikin Research Foundation. During the twenty years prior to his death, he conducted research in the fields of nutrition, exercise, and degenerative diseases, along with doing clinical studies that corroborated the various concepts he developed. Pritikin long advocated walking as the ultimate exercise and included it in his diet and exercise programs.

He was granted more than two dozen patents and was an Honorary Fellow of the International Academy of Preventive Medicine. He was also coauthor of the best-selling *Live Longer Now.*

! DR. JAMES RIPPE

Dr. James Rippe is co-director of the Exercise Physiology and Nutrition Laboratory at the University of Massachusetts Medical School. He is also the Director of the American Health Fitness Institute and of the Rockport Walking Institute. Dr. Rippe has written several walking books, including *The Book of Fitness Walking.*

❗ ROCKPORT WALKING INSTITUTE

The Rockport Walking Institute, located in Marlboro, Massachusetts, was developed to study walking and the effects it has on human beings. Its most notable project to date was the Robert Sweetgall/Rockport Walk around the country to learn about the many effects of long-distance walking. Rockport has brought a great deal of practical information to the domestic marketplace through their various studies on walking. From walking at home and work, to walking for people over fifty, to hiking and backpacking, Rockport is the premier walking shoe company in America.

❗ TOM RUTLAND

A devout exerciser for over twenty years, Tom Rutland conceived, designed, and tested the Exerstrider™. The Exerstrider is a pair of modified ski poles used for walking. Through using them, force is exerted by major muscle groups in the upper body.

Sidelined by a running injury, he conceived of the Exerstrider while he was "ski-striding," a training technique used by Rutland to prepare for the cross-country skiing season. During the ensuing two and a half years, he would go on to develop the Exerstrider.

Currently, Tom lives in Madison, Wisconsin with his wife and Exerstrides four to six miles a day.

❗ ROBERT SWEETGALL

Founder of Creative Walking, Inc., Robert Sweetgall has walked across America four times. In 1986, he walked a distance around the U.S. of 11,208 miles in a period of one year.

After quitting his job with DuPont in 1969, he realized the value of good health and exercise. He wanted some sort of career in health.

In 1981 he founded The Foundation for the Development of Cardiovascular Health and organized a school lecture tour. Intent on walking across America to create a new walking awareness, Sweetgall solicited sponsors; ultimately Rockport and GoreTex acquiesced, and Sweetgall was on his feet.

64. *Robert Sweetgall, the most famous long-distance walker in the United States, is the author of numerous books and founder and president of Creative Walking, Inc.*

63. *Tom Rutland, developer of the Exer-strider™. It looks like cross-country skiing without the skis, and has a lot of the benefit of cross-country skiing, too.*

Today, his primary interest is in helping students get healthy — both in body and mind — through walking with his walking company.

Conclusion

If you have lived long enough, you have seen a lot. You know what's out there. You know what's not.

You've taken some knocks. And you've dished some out. You learned to understand that nobody's perfect. And the best you can do is to do your best.

If you have lived long enough, you've realized that the world is no longer a round ball on a dusty metal pedestal. The world is bigger. It's complicated. It's unfair.

You used to think you could change the world. You used to think that you could do anything you wanted. You used to believe in Santa Claus.

You've been around. You know what is real and what is not so real. You know there is only one thing you can count on in this world.

Yourself.

You made it. And you've realized that only you can change.

You're getting older. Wiser. You take care of yourself.

But the kids start to say that you're old and grey and over the hill . . .

Tell them that you WALKED IT.

For the pure joy of it.

65. *"See you on the road . . ."*

APPENDIX

Walking Groups and Associations Around the U.S.

Following is a listing of some of the major walking organizations around the country. When contacting them, ask about their walking program. If it does not suit you, ask them for a referral to other groups in the area. You probably will find that local walking groups are aware of each other.

ALABAMA

Riverchase Galleria
3000 Riverchase Galleria, Suite 905
Birmingham, AL 35244

Ann Bibber
2301 Airport Blvd.
Mobile, AL 36606

Capital City Wanderers
913 Smith Street
Montgomery, AL 36113

ALASKA

Sierra Club
Alaska Chapter
P.O. Box 100767
Anchorage, AK 99510

Lyle Perrigo
1921 Congress Circle #B
Anchorage, AK 99507

ARIZONA

Walkabout Arizona
P.O. Box 5926
Glendale, AZ 85312

Prescott Walkers
1150 Smokie
Prescott, AZ 86301

Arizona Walker's Club
812 West Port Au Prince
Phoenix, AZ 85023

Walk in the Park
5301 East Grant Road
Tucson, AZ 85733

ARKANSAS

Little Rock Razorback Volksmarchers
Thomas Recreation Center
314 CSG/SSRR
Little Rock AFB, AR 72099-5000

CALIFORNIA
California Walkers
John Kelly
1024 3rd Street
Santa Monica, CA 90403

Footloose
1413 South Nutwood Street
Anaheim, CA 92804

Berkeley Hiking Club
P.O. Box 147
Berkeley, CA 94701

Walk-A-Way
Buena Park Mall
8308 on the Mall
Buena Park, CA 90620

Merry Walkers Club
26127 Village 26
Camarillo, CA 93010

Starlight Hiking Club
165 East Milann Street
Chula Vista, CA 92010

REI Walkers
5961 Sunrise Blvd.
Citrus Heights, CA 95610

Wayne Glusker
20351 Bollinger Road
Cupertino, CA 95014

Apple Striders
20525 Mariani Avenue
M/S/26AZ
Cupertino, CA 95014

Joy Walkers
47 Esparito Avenue
Fremont, CA 94539

Glendale Go-Getters
Glendale Galleria
2148 Glendale Galleria
Glendale, CA 91210

Fast Walkers
24301 Southland Drive, B-1
Hayward, CA 94545

Easy Striders Walking Club
P.O. Box 2714
Huntington Beach, CA 92647

Sunday Strollers
4370 Fairlawn Drive
La Canada, CA 91011

Sierra Club
3550 West Sixth Street
Los Angeles, CA 90020

Wilder's Walkers
P.O. Box 46212
Los Angeles, CA 90046

Montclair Walking Group
9831 Bel Aire Avenue
Montclair, CA 91763

Walk For Life
Palm Desert Town Center
72840 Hwy. 111
Palm Desert, CA 92260

Palo Alto Striding Club
Palo Alto Recreation Center
1305 Middlefield Road
Palo Alto, CA 94301

Walkers Club of Los Angeles
610 Woodward Blvd.
Pasadena, CA 91107

Sacramento Orienteering Club
8352 Sutter Buttes Way
Sacramento, CA 95825

Walkabout International
835 5th Avenue
San Diego, CA 92101

Goldengate Walkers
106 Sanchez Street #107
San Francisco, CA 94114

Sierra Club
Outing Club
730 Polk Street
San Francisco, CA 94109

Five A.M. Wake Up Walkers
Steve Joyner
801 Sutter Street #106
San Francisco, CA 94109

San Mateo Walkers
106 East 25th Street
San Mateo, CA 94403

Santa Barbara Sport Walkers
P.O. Box 21936
Santa Barbara, CA 93105

Walk For Your Life
Camarillo Recreation Center
100 East Camarillo
Santa Barbara, CA 93101

Walk For Health
2442 232nd Street
Torrance, CA 90501

COLORADO

Mallwalkers
Crossroads Mall
1600 28th Street
Boulder, CO 80301

Mall Walkers
Chapel Hills Mall
1710 Briargate Blvd.
Colorado Springs, CO 80920

Front Range Walkers
2261 Glencoe Street
Denver, CO 80207

CONNECTICUT

Hartford YMCA Walkers Club
160 Jewell Street
Hartford, CT 06103

Bill Mongovan
12 Doubling Road
Greenwich, CT 06830

DELAWARE

Dover Mall Walkers Club
3054 Dover Mall
Dover, DE 19901

DISTRICT OF COLUMBIA

American Hiking Society
1015 31st Street
Washington, DC 20007

FLORIDA

Florida Walkers
Bob Fine
4223 Palm Forest Drive North
Delray Beach, FL 33445

Wake Up and Walk
Panama City Mall
2150 Cove Blvd.
Panama City, FL 32405

Tampa Bay Walkers
James McCarthy
12308 North 27th Street
Tampa Bay, FL 33612

Roberts Adult Center
Dept. of Leisure Services
1330 50th Avenue North
St. Petersburg, FL 33703

Walk for the Health of It
Winter Haven Mall
P.O. Box 1729
Winter Haven, FL 33880

GEORGIA

Healthworks Walking Club
One Coca-Cola Plaza
Atlanta, GA 30313

Walkers Club of Georgia
Dr. Bill Farrel
818 Peachtree Center South
Atlanta, GA 30303

Stride in Style Walking Clubs
Lenox Square
3393 Peachtree Road
Atlanta, GA 30342

Walk For Life
Columbus Square Mall
3050 Macon Road
Columbus, GA 31906

HAWAII

Hawaii Walkers
708 Hausten Street
Honolulu, HI 92826-3041

IDAHO

Happy Hoofers
P.O. Box 1435
Boise, ID 83701

ILLINOIS

Chicago Walkersize
1246 West Fullerton
Chicago, IL 60614

Chicago Walkers
111 West Butterfield Road
Elmhurst, IL 60126

Take-A-Walk Walking Club
2112 North Clark Street
Chicago, IL 60614

Lakeshore Walking Club
1515 Howard Street
Evanston, IL 60202

Toime Square Mall Walkers
Toime Square Mall
42nd and Broadway
Mt. Vernon, IL 62864

Pacemakers
West Chicago Park District
157 West Washington
West Chicago, IL 60185

Woodstock Walkers
City of Woodstock
Recreation Division
P.O. Box 190
121 West Calhoun Street
Woodstock, IL 60098

INDIANA

Columbus Wellness Walkers
2454 S. 475 W.
Columbus, IN 47201

Sam Bell
Assembly Hall
Indiana University
Bloomington, IN 47401

Indianapolis Hiking Club
6847 Brill Road
Indianapolis, IN 46207

Westfield Walkers
326 Main Street
Westfield, IN 46030

IOWA

Paul Schneider
Siouxand YMCA
722 Nebraska Street
Sioux City, IA 51101

College Square Mall Walkers
College Square Mall
6301 University Avenue
Cedar Falls, IA 50613

Sierra Club
3500 Kingman Blvd.
Des Moines, IA 50311

Southern Hills Mall Walkers
Southern Hills Mall
4400 Sergeant Road
Sioux City, IA 51106

KANSAS

Kansas City Walkers
c/o Don Lawrence
4500 West 107th Street
Overland Park, KS 66207

Kansas Jay Walkers
P.O. Box 3136
Ft. Leavenworth, KS 66027

White Lakes Mall Walkers
White Lakes Mall
3600 Topeka Blvd.
Topeka, KS 66611

KENTUCKY

Lexington Striders Walking Club
Division of Parks and Recreation
525 North Upper Street
Lexington, KY 40508

Kentucky Walkers
Jefferson Mall
4801-302 Outer Loop
Louisville, KY 40219

LOUISIANA

Baton Rouge Striders
7656 Jefferson Hwy.
Baton Rouge, LA 70809

New Orleans Walkers
4236 South Roman Street
New Orleans, LA 70125

Plaza Mall Walkers
Plaza in Lake Forest
5700 Read Blvd.
New Orleans, LA 70127

MAINE

Paris Hill Early Walkers
P.O. Box 42
Paris, ME 04271

Maine Mall Miler
364 Maine Mall Road
South Portland, ME 04106

MARYLAND

Baltimore Walkers
4120 Balmoral Circle
Baltimore, MD 21208

Brisk Walking Is No Sweat
Baltimore City Health Dept.
303 East Fayette Street, 2nd Floor
Baltimore, MD 21203

Rise and Shine Walking Club
5434 Vantage Point Road
Columbia, MD 21044

Fast Trackers Walking Club
Montgomery County Health Dept.
100 Maryland Avenue, Room 121
Rockville, MD 20850

MASSACHUSETTS

Legislator's Walking Club
Rep. Alfred Saggese
State House, Room 155
Boston, MA 02133

Brookline Racewalkers Club
P.O. Box 955
Brookline, MA 02146

New England Walkers
83 Riverside Avenue
Concord, MA 01742

Early Birds
245 Franklin Street
Holyoke, MA 01040

Walk Fitness
Cape Cod YMCA
76 Enterprise Road
Hyannis, MA 02601

Stepping Healthy
Lawrence Memorial Hospital
Community Relations Dept.
171 Governors Avenue
Medford, MA 02155

MICHIGAN
Arborland Heart and Sole
794 Peninsula
Ann Arbor, MI 48105

Washtenlaw Walkers
Briarwood Mall
P.O. Box 8645
Ann Arbor, MI 48107

Carrier Creek Walkers
7332 Creek Side Drive
Lansing, MI 48917

Wolverine Pacers
c/o Frank Alongi
26530 Woodshire Avenue
Dearborn Heights, MI 48127

West Michigan Walkers
10630 52nd Street SE
Lowell, MI 49331

West Bloomfield Walkers Club
West Bloomfield Parks and
  Recreation
3325 Middlebelt
West Bloomfield, MI 48033

MINNESOTA
River Bend Striders
P.O. Box 007
Cleveland, MN 56017

St. Paul Hiking Club
1767 Maple Lane
St. Paul, MN 55113

MISSOURI
Mall Walkers
Capital Mall
3600 Country Club Drive
Jefferson City, MO 65101

Missouri Marching Mules
4800 Weber Road
St. Louis, MO 63123

Battlefield Mall Walkers
101 Battlefield Mall
Springfield, MO 65804

MONTANA
Big Sky Wanderers
2209 Central Avenue West
Great Falls, MT 59404

NEBRASKA
Lincoln Volkssport Club
1519 North 58th Street
Lincoln, NE 68505

Omaha Walking Club
2402 South 40th Street
Omaha, NE 68132

NEVADA
Lake Tahoe Walkers Alliance
P.O. Box 8679
Incline Village, NV 89450

Las Vegas High Rollers and Strollers
P.O. Box 30153
N Las Vegas, NV 89030-0153

Las Vegas Walkers
P.O. Box 623
Mercury, NV 89023

Meadowwood Miler
1 Meadowood Mall Circle
Reno, NV 89502

NEW HAMPSHIRE

Seacoast Striders
P.O. Box 3151 Omni Mall
Portsmouth, NH 03801

NEW JERSEY

Livingston Mall Walkers
Livingston Mall
112 Eisenhower Pkwy.
Livingston, NJ 07039

Master Walker
Regency House, Room 254
Pompton Plains, NJ 07444

New Jersey Striders
P.O. Box 742
Madison, NJ 07940

NEW MEXICO

Heart and Sole
Coronado Center
1100 Coronado Center
Albuquerque, NM 87110

Mall Walkers
Villa Linda Mall
4250 Cerrillo Road
Santa Fe, NM 87505

NEW YORK

Plaza Pacers
Empire State Plaza
c/o Health Works and NY State Health
    Dept.
Corning Tower, Room 1084
Albany, NY 12237

Pyramid Mall of Ithaca Walking Club
40 Catherwood Road
Ithaca, NY 14850

Balboa's Walking Club
140 West 79th Street
Suite 10A
New York, NY 10024

Walkers Club of America
Box M
Livingston Manor, NY 12758

Walk For Life
Settlement Health and Medical
    Services
314 East 104th Street
New York, NY 10029

Mall Walkers
American Heart Assoc. of Rochester
874 Edgemere Drive
Rochester, NY 14612

Woodstock Walking Club
132 Hutchin Hill Road
Shady, NY 12479

YMCA Volksmarck Walking Group
YMCA
340 Montgomery Street
Syracuse, NY 13202

NORTH CAROLINA

Southeastern Masters
P.O. Box 590
Raleigh, NC 27602

Chapel Hill Walking Group
Chapel Hill Recreation Dept.
Plant Road
Chapel Hill, NC 27514

Hearts and Soul
Hwy. 29 North
Concord, NC 28025

Backwoods Orienteering Club
904 Dorothea Drive
Raleigh, NC 27603

Winston Wanderers
P.O. Box 15013
Winston-Salem, NC 27113

OHIO

Ohio Racewalker
3184 Summit Street
Columbus, OH 43202

3H Walkers
Chapel Hill Mall
Britten and Home Roads
Akron, OH 44310

American Walkers Association
3223 Day Court
Cincinnati, OH 45238

Cincinnati Walking Club
11284 Chester Road
Cincinnati, OH 45246

Cleveland Walkers Club
4202 Archwood Avenue
Cleveland, OH 44109

German Village Wander Volk
34 East Gates Street
Columbus, OH 43206

Dayton Walking Club
AMC Branch
Box 33598
Dayton, OH 45433

Mall Walkers
Southwick Shopping Center
2024 South Reynolds Road
Toledo, OH 43614

OKLAHOMA

Frontier Walkers
P.O. Box 24122
Oklahoma City, OK 73124

Oklahoma Fitness Walkers
2712 NW 48
Oklahoma City, OK 73112

Tulsa Walkers
6764 East 90th Avenue, South
Tulsa, OK 74133

OREGON

Ponderosa Pathfinders
905 NE Franklin
Bend, OR 97701

Striders
155 High Street
Eugene, OR 97405

Wednesday Walkers
1200 Mira Mar Avenue #906
Medford, OR 97504

Rose City Roamers
13737 SE Ellis Street
Portland, OR 97236

Mall Walkers
831 Lancaster Drive NE
Salem, OR 97301

PENNSYLVANIA

Happy Feet Walking Club
Smith Kline and French Laboratories
P.O. Box 1539
King of Prussia, PA 19406

Park City Walkers
713 Columbia Avenue
Lancaster, PA 17603

American Youth Hostels
Delaware Valley Council
35 South 3rd Street
Philadelphia, PA 19106

American Youth Hostels
Pittsburgh Council
6300 5th Avenue
Pittsburgh, PA 15232

Mall Walkers
South Hills Health Systems
P.O. Box 18119
Pittsburgh, PA 15326

Sierra Club
Northeastern Pennsylvania Group
P.O. Box 1311
Scranton, PA 18501

RHODE ISLAND
Warwick Wanderers
975 Sandy Lane
Warwick, RI 02886

SOUTH CAROLINA
500 Mile Club
Anderson Mall
3131 North Main
Anderson, SC 29621

Northwoods Mall Walkers
Trident Regional Medical Center
9330 Medical Plaza Drive
Charleston, SC 29418

The Mall Walkers
Haywood Mall
700 Haywood Road
Greenville, SC 29607

SOUTH DAKOTA
Bradley Knudson
811 University
Spearfish, SD 57783

Empire Mall Walkers Club
Sioux Valley Wellness Center
3600 West 43rd
Sioux Falls, SD 57106

TENNESSEE
Smoky Mountain Hiking Club
P.O. Box 1454
Knoxville, TN 37901

Pacers Program
Hickory Ridge Mall
6075 Winchester
Memphis, TN 38115

TEXAS
River City Walkers
2705 McCullough
Austin, TX 78703

Fort Bliss Wind Walkers
5222 Marcillus Avenue
El Paso, TX 79924

West Texas Trail Walkers
P.O. Box 17126
Fort Worth, TX 76102

Dallas Trekkers
406 Atherton
Garland, TX 75043

Space City Trail Trotters
11622 Old Telegraph Road
Houston, TX 77067

Morning Milers
McCreeless Mall
4100 South New Braunfels
San Antonio, TX 78223

UTAH

Walk-N-Talk Club
Weber County Mental Health Center
2650 Lincoln Avenue
Ogden, UT 84401

Sierra Club
177 E 900 S
Suite 102
Salt Lake City, UT 84102

VERMONT

Walk For Joy
University Mall
155 Dorset Street
South Burlington, VT 05401

Wellness Program
State of Vermont
Department of Health
1193 North Avenue
P.O. Box 70
Burlington, VT 05402

VIRGINIA

Potomac Valley Walkers
3466 Roberts Lane
North Arlington, VA 22207

Peninsula Pathfinders of Virginia
212 Prince James Drive
Hampton, VA 23669

Mall Walkers
Lewis-Gale Hospital
1900 Electric Road
Salem, VA 24153

Lynnhaven Fit-Print Walkers
701 Lynnhaven Parkway
Suite 1068
Virginia Beach, VA 23452

WASHINGTON

Pacific Pacers
6633 NE Windemere Road
Seattle, WA 98115

Interlaken Trailblazers
P.O. Box 70068
Bellevue, WA 98007

Heart Walkers
Everett Mall
1402 SE Everett Mall Way
Everett, WA 98208

Emerald City Wanderers
P.O. Box 16621
Seattle, WA 98116

Seattle Striders
P.O. Box 27573
Seattle, WA 98125

Evergreen Wanderers
P.O. Box 111943
Tacoma, WA 98411

WEST VIRGINIA

Kanawha Trail Club
P.O. Box 4474
Charleston, WV 25364

Walk For Life Club
100 Grand Center Mall
Parkersburg, WV 26101

WISCONSIN

Badger Walkers
6589 North Crestwood Drive
Milwaukee, WI 53209

Sierra Club
111 King Street
Madison, WI 53706

Walkers Group
Plymouth Senior Center
910 East Clifford Street
Plymouth, WI 53073

Wausau Center Mall Walkers Club
C-302 Wausau Center Mall
Wausau, WI 54401

Glossary

Achilles tendinitis. Inflammation of the Achilles tendon.

Achilles tendon. The tendon connecting the back of the legs to the muscles of the calf.

Aerobic organisms. Living creatures that require an external source of oxygen to survive.

Aerobic walking. Walking to stimulate the efficiency of oxygen intake into the body.

Aerobicise. A recent exercise movement involving a series of fast, repetitive exercises that maintain a steady heart rate and oxygen intake.

Altimeter. An instrument for measuring the height above a given level.

AMS. Acute Mountain Sickness.

Anaerobic. The ability to live or grow without air or free oxygen.

Anxiety. A feeling characterized by uneasiness and apprehension about normal day-to-day events. Anxiety may be helped by walking regularly.

Arch. Part of the foot, made up of five bones, that serves as the body's natural shock absorber, alignment mechanism, and body support.

Arm Swing. The motion of the arm that maintains momentum when the opposite foot is back stepping.

Arteriosclerosis. The abnormal thickening and loss of flexibility of the walls of the arteries.

Arthritis. The inflammation of the joints.

Barometer. An instrument for measuring atmospheric pressure.

Blood Pressure. The pressure exerted by the blood against the walls of the blood vessels.

Calf. The fleshy part of the leg below the knee.

Callus. Thick and hardened skin resulting from continued friction.

Calorie. A unit used for measuring the energy produced by food when oxidized by the body.

Cancer. Abnormal and rapid cell growth.

Cardiovascular. Referring to the heart and its blood vessels.

Cerebral Edema. An abnormal accumulation of fluid in the brain.

Cholesterol. A fat-like substance found in animal products and dairy byproducts.

Chronic Fitness Dropout. The tendency for people engaging in a fitness program ultimately not to stick with it. In fact, true fitness is a lifelong process.

Cirrhosis. An abnormal buildup of body tissue. Typically found in the livers of long-term alcohol abusers.

Cool-downs. Refers to the process of stretching after a walking routine to prevent a buildup of lactic acid and stiffness, which create soreness in the muscles.

Cramp. A powerful contraction of the muscle. Tends to occur due to lack of aerobic fitness or dehydration.

Cybex. A type of muscle strengthening equipment.

Depression. A neurotic or psychotic condition characterized by feelings of despair, hopelessness, and often thoughts of suicide.

Diabetes. A disease characterized by excess sugar in the blood and urine, hunger, and thirst.

Dog Repellent. A benign chemical formula used to quell dog attacks directed towards human beings.

Emerson, Ralph Waldo. American essayist, poet, and philosopher. Born in 1803 and died in 1882.

Endurance Walking. The equivalent of marathon walking and beyond. An example: Robert Sweetgall, who walked 11,208 miles around the U.S. in one year, is an endurance walker.

EVA. Ethylene vinyl acetate. A soft, lightweight material commonly used for cushioning the midsoles of walking shoes.

Exercise Sandals. Special sandals with supportive straps designed for walking and other low-impact movement.

Exerstriders. A pair of walking sticks, actually modified ski poles, designed for Exerstriding.

Exerstriding. A technique of walking, jogging, or bounding while using a pair of walking sticks (modified ski poles).

Fanny Pack. A small pack that straps around the waist.

Fat Caliper. A tweezer-like device used for measuring the amount of fat by pinching it on the epidermis.

Fleecewear. A mid-layer of clothing that serves as an insulator and draws moisture away from the body.

Footbed. What the foot rests on; usually a sock liner or an insert.

James Fixx. Runner and writer who died in the 1980s of heart failure.

Groin. The fold where the abdomen joins either thigh.

Hamstring. One of the tendons in back of the knee.

Heat Stroke. An overheating of the body. Symptoms include lightheadedness, hot-feeling skin, weakness, nausea, faintness, and extreme thirst.

Heavyhands. Hand weights used during walking and running to increase the metabolic benefit.

Heel Counter. The firm cup at the back of the shoe that wraps around the heel and provides lateral (outside) and medial (inside) stability.

Heel Cradle. A part of the footbed that encircles the base of the heel, adding stability and comfort.

Heel Cup. A heel counter; also refers to a device added to the inside of the shoe for extra cushioning and protection.

Heel Cushion. A device inserted in the footbed to absorb shock to the foot.

Heel Plug. An insert into the midsole or outsole, under the heel.

Heel Spur. An inflammation of a ligament under the heel. If you walk more than you are physically prepared to or over-stretch it in some other activity, this ligament may become partially detached from the bone.

Heel Stabilizer. A motion-control device that keeps the rear of the foot steady.

Hippocrates. Greek physician, often called the Father of Medicine.

Hypothermia. Subnormal body temperature.

Insole. The insert or sock lining on which the foot rests.

Iodine. A chemical element used as an antiseptic.

Jogger's Ankle. A new term in the orthopedic field; refers to the sprains that account for three-quarters of joggers' ankle injuries.

Last. The mold on which shoes are wrapped.

Midsole. The cushioning material between the insole and the bottom of the shoe.

Massage. The rubbing and kneading of the body with the hands to stimulate blood flow and relieve bodily tension.

Moleskin. A adhesive layer of cloth used to reduce the direct amount of friction placed on the skin.

Natural Stride. A stride that comes naturally to you. To find yours, lift your leg and fall forward. The step you take to save yourself is your natural stride.

Nausea. A feeling of sickness in the stomach.

Nautilus. A type of fitness equipment that varies the weight resistance for the user.

"No pain no gain." A contemporary exercise myth that says that unless you feel pain when you exercise, you will not achieve significant results.

Noisemaker. Referring to a whistle, a clap, or a horn to scare attacking dogs.

Notched Heel Collar. A notch cut into the back of the shoe collar to prevent irritation of the heel and Achilles tendon.

Obesity. An unhealthy condition of being overweight.

Orthotic. A scientifically designed device used to correct aberrations in the feet.

Osteoporosis. A disease in which bone mass reduces and porous and brittle bones develop.

Outsole. The very bottom of the shoe — the surface that comes in contact with ground. A flared outsole (sometimes called a flared midsole) typically found on running shoes widens below the foot for added stability.

Outerwear. The outermost layer of clothing worn to protect against wind, rain, and snow.

Overpronation. A condition in which the feet turn too far inward when walking; also called pigeon-toed.

Oxygen debt. The state when your body is not getting oxygen to your extremities fast enough, resulting in a feeling of sluggishness.

Oxygen-Transport Capacity. The amount of oxygen that each heartbeat delivers to the rest of the body.

Pace. A step in one's walking stride.

Pedestrian Commuting. Commuting to work or other destinations by walking.

Pedometer. A mechanical device used to record the number of steps taken.

Physical Contact Sport. A sport involving body to body contact with another participant.

Pneumonia. Inflammation of the lungs.

Polypropylene Fleece. The first layer of clothing designed to wick away moisture from the skin.

Positive Stress. Also known is eustress. An example: walking up a hill.

Posture. One's standing position.

Pulmonary Edema. An accumulation of fluid in the lungs.

Pulse Monitor. An electronic device that straps onto your wrist and measures your heartbeat.

Quadriceps. The large muscles at the front of the thigh.

Rash. An eruption of spots on the skin.

Recipe of Four. Walk four times a week for one hour at four miles per hour.

Rockport Corporation. A U.S. company dedicated to the advancement of footwear and walking.

Roller Blade™. A variation of roller skating but with just one linear set of wheels on each skate.

Runner's Fatigue. Pain developed by running after a given period of time; characterized by soreness throughout the body.

Saddle. The flap that goes over the top of the foot, near the laces, to add arch support and stability.

Self-esteem. One's sense of worth and validity in the world.

Sesmoiditis. A clinical term for pain in the ball of the foot, caused when tiny bones in the foot below the first metatarsals become bruised.

Shank. A piece of firm material that runs from the ball of the foot to the heel between the insole and the midsole for added arch support.

Shin. The front part of the leg between the knee and the ankle.

Snowshoe. A racket-shaped frame of wood crisscrossed with strips of leather that prevent sinking while walking in the snow.

Sock Liner. The top layer of an insole that is sometimes contoured; it can be removable or treated with anti-bacterial chemicals.

Sonic Jacket. A specially made brand of jacket for carrying portable stereo equipment.

Spot Reduction. A myth concerning the localized reduction of fat. It cannot be done.

Stress. A mental or physical strain on the body.

Stretch in Motion. The process of stretching while you are walking.

Stride. The length of one's natural step.

Sweetgall, Robert. Famous endurance walker.

Thoreau, Henry David. American naturalist and writer; *Walden* is one of his most famous works. He was born in 1817 and died in 1862.

Treadmill. An exercise device in which the tread determines the speed, intensity, and duration of the walk.

Upper. The part of the shoe that rises above the insole; it is generally made of leather, canvas, or nylon.

Walking Attitude. Simple, pure, free.

The Walking Magazine. A periodical on walking and walking events. For more information write to: 711 Boylston Street, Boston, MA 02116.

Walking Marathon. A twenty-six mile walk.

Walkman™. A portable stereo/cassette player.

Wedge. The thicker part of the midsole that makes the heel higher than the ball of the foot.

Weston, Edward Payson. Considered the most famous race walker in modern history. He was born in 1839 and died in 1929.

Bibliography

Balboa, Deena and Balboa, David. *Walk For Life*. New York: Perigee Books, 1990.

Finch, Robert. "Expectations." *The Walking Magazine*, October/November 1987, p. 88.

Goldman, H.H. *Review of General Psychiatry*. Norwalk, Connecticut: Appleton and Lange, 1988.

Hesson, James., and Lon, Seiger. *Walking For Health*. Dubuque, Iowa: Wm. C. Brown Publishers, 1990.

Neeves, Robert, Ph.D.; Sweetgall, Robert; and Whiteley, Roba, MS, RD. *Walking Off Weight*. Calyton Creative Publishing Incorporated, 1989.

Pullen, William, Dr. Telephone conversation on August 7, 1991.

Rippe, James M. *Complete Book of Fitness Walking*. New York: Prentice-Hall Press, 1990.

Rutland, Tom. Numerous telephone conversations, August 1991 to October 1991.

Schwartz, Leonard, M.D. *Heavyhands Walking*. Emmaus, Pennsylvania: Rodale Press, 1987.

Sweetgall, Robert. *Fitness Walking*. New York: Perigee Books, 1985.

Sweetgall, Robert. Telephone conversation, August 13, 1991.

Thoreau, Henry David. "Walking." *Atlantic Monthly*, 1862.

Yanker, Gary. *Complete Book of Exercise Walking*. Chicago: Contemporary Books, 1983.

"The Road Not Taken"
Robert Frost

Two roads diverged in a yellow wood,
And sorry I could not travel both
And be one traveler, long I stood
And looked down one as far as I could
To where it bent in the undergrowth

Then took the other, as just as fair,
And having perhaps the better claim,
Because it was grassy and wanted wear
Though as for that the passing there
Had worn them really about the same,

And both that morning equally lay
In leaves no step had trodden black,
Oh, I kept the first for another day!
Yet knowing how way leads on to way,
I doubted if I should ever come back.

I shall be telling this with a sigh
Somewhere ages and ages hence
Two roads diverged in a wood, and I —
I took the one less traveled by,
And that has made all the difference.

(Reprinted from *New England Anthology of Robert Frost Poems,* courtesy of Washington Square Press.)

Index